"*A Feather and a Fork* is more than a cookbook full of mouthwatering recipes—it's a story map, a love song, and a survival guide. Indigenous chef Crystal Wahpepah serves up food as ceremony and resistance, weaving memory, community, and legacy into every dish. This is ancestral knowledge coming to you straight outta Oakland's Fruitvale, where she was raised—reminding us that resistance is sometimes a responsibility, and that reclaiming your food, your land, and your story can be an act of love."

—PETER BRATT, Peabody Award winner, Emmy-nominated film producer, writer, and director

▲▲▲

"Driven by a love for our Indigenous culture, community, and resistance, Chef Crystal Wahpepah has cataloged an important collection of recipes that takes us on a powerful journey across the vast landscape of Indigenous Resurgence. These recipes, ingredients, and stories will be studied for years to come as they guide us into the next chapter of Indigenous cooking and cuisine in the Americas. Chef Crystal lovingly brings us into her life and community, and provides a profound glimpse into what has made her one of the most driven and successful Indigenous chefs in our generation."

—White Mountain Apache and Dine' chef NEPHI CRAIG

▲▲▲

"Chef Crystal Wahpepah's new cookbook is nothing short of a masterpiece. Each page of *A Feather and a Fork* radiates with the care, respect, and deep love that Chef Crystal holds for our traditional foods, our ancestors, and our future generations. It is both a celebration and a reclamation—a vibrant tapestry woven with ancestral knowledge, culinary artistry, and the kind of fierce pride only someone rooted deeply in their culture can bring to life. As a fellow Native chef, I am filled with pride and gratitude. This book is more than recipes—it's medicine, it's memory, it is *ours*. Crystal has given us a gift that will nourish our people for generations to come."

—Citizen Potawatomi Nation chef LORETTA BARRETT ODEN, author of *Corn Dance: Inspired First American Cuisine*

A FEATHER AND A FORK

125 Intertribal Dishes from an Indigenous Food Warrior

CRYSTAL WAHPEPAH

WITH AMY PAIGE CONDON

Photographs by Clay Williams

RODALE

NEW YORK

Rodale Books
An imprint of Random House
A division of Penguin Random House LLC
1745 Broadway, New York, NY 10019
rodalebooks.com | *randomhousebooks.com*
penguinrandomhouse.com

Rodale & Plant with colophon is a registered trademark of Penguin Random House LLC.
Library of Congress Cataloging-in-Publication Data
Names: Wahpepah, Crystal author | Condon, Amy Paige author
Title: A feather and a fork / by Crystal Wahpepah with Amy Paige Condon.
Description: First edition. | New York, NY : Rodale, [2026] | Includes bibliographical references and index.
Identifiers: LCCN 2025024518 (print) | LCCN 2025024519 (ebook) | ISBN 9780593736036 hardcover | ISBN 9780593736043 ebook
Subjects: LCSH: Indians of North America—Food | Indian cooking | Cooking, American | Cooking—America | LCGFT: Cookbooks
Classification: LCC E98.F7 W347 2026 (print) | LCC E98.F7 (ebook) | DDC 641.59/297—dc23/eng/20250807
LC record available at https://lccn.loc.gov/2025024518
LC ebook record available at https://lccn.loc.gov/2025024519
ISBN 978-0-593-73603-6
Ebook ISBN 978-0-593-73604-3

Printed in China

9 8 7 6 5 4 3 2 1

First Edition

BOOK TEAM:
Editor: Dervla Kelly
Editorial assistant: Emi Harris
Creative Director: Jenny Davis
Art Director: Lynne Yeamans
Designer: Lisa Schneller Bieser
Managing Editor: Allie Fox
Production manager: Richard Elman
Copyeditor: Deborah Weiss Geline
Proofreaders: Leda Scheintaub, Kate Bolen, Pam Rehm
Indexer: Elizabeth T. Parson

(white texture watercolor paper) xamtiw/Adobe Stock (used throughout book); (abstract wall background with green paint roller strokes) Mr Twister/Adobe Stock (used throughout book); (grey paint brush strokes as a frame on white background) Mr Twister/Adobe Stock (used throughout book); (crumpled paper texture vector background, white wrinkled sheet EPS10) Angela Ksen/Adobe Stock (used in border on page 30); *The Red Road* by Jason Dobbs (mural in photograph on page 164); photographs on wall in the Intertribal Friendship House photo on page 164 by Irwin Lewis and Bryan Spencer

The authorized representative in the EU for product safety and compliance is Penguin Random House Ireland, Morrison Chambers, 32 Nassau Street, Dublin D02 YH68, Ireland.
https://eu-contact.penguin.ie

To my mother, Beverly Wahpepah; my sister, Mercedes Wahpepah, and my niece, Serena Osife—you all left us way too early. We went through so much together, and I miss you every day.

Mercedes, I hope to make our children proud.

—CW

CONTENTS

3 GAME AND FISH
Wiiyaathi Chakisii Memeethaki 195

CREATOR

Every day when I enter Wahpepah's Kitchen, I arrive early, before everyone else, so that I have time to take it all in, center myself, and affirm my intentions. I speak to the heirloom seeds I have saved in jars on my shelves because they are sacred gifts, then I say my prayers. And so, it seems only fitting to begin this book with a prayer.

> *Kisihiyaata (Dear Creator), May the words on these pages, the languages spoken and the recipes shared, be the root of mutual understanding and the seed of healing, not just for my circle but for all who pick up this book, read it, and cook from it. May your body and spirit be nourished, and may we find a deeper connection to the land and one another through my sharing my story.*

FOREWORD

Food is one of those things so essential, like the air we breathe, sometimes we can forget that it's there, and what it's there for—its uses and its histories and the land it comes from, the people who took care of and lived on and cultivated that land for millennia. Too often we haven't valued what the Indigenous peoples of the Americas were doing before Europeans arrived on North American shores. But it's a difficult thing to try to get back what has not only been forgotten but purposefully wiped out over hundreds of years. It takes years of hard work and dedication, building relationships and spending time with people who still carry that knowledge. We are lucky to have the kinds of people willing to do the work to gift us with such knowledge.

Reading this book, I felt an overwhelming sense of hope for the future of Oakland, California, and for indigenous foodways being cultivated and restored all over this country. Like the tremendously talented, heart-and-soul-driven chef Crystal Wahpepah, I too am a Native person born and raised in Oakland. We also share that the Native American Health Center played a crucial part in shaping our lives. I worked at NAHC for almost a decade. I met my wife, Kateri, there. Started writing my first novel, *There There,* there. I was there when—as Crystal recounts in the brilliant and disarmingly honest introduction to this book—she was first asked to cater for the GOTL (Gathering of the Lodges) event at the center. I'd designed the T-shirts for the event—her first major catering gig. And I'm honored to say that I was one of the first people to taste some of the food from the recipes contained in this book.

I think it's safe to say that most people living in the twenty-first century have a complicated relationship with food. Just, for example, I recently read that, without meaning to, we ingest a credit card's worth of microplastics a week. Maybe this isn't entirely true, or not entirely true of all people, but it's true enough. We are removed from what we are putting in our bodies. Removed from the growth of food, removed from its preparation, removed from the knowledge of what food provides us. This book is a gift, allowing us precious information about why we should be eating certain foods and how we should be thinking about the stories behind the foods we should be eating. Sometimes when we talk about the "shoulds" of eating, it seems like we're talking about chewing straight raw kale, and that if it's not downright punishing, it definitely won't be an enjoyable experience. That's why books like this are important.

The food in these recipes is by and large good for you, and also delicious. The two need not be exclusive. And this book gives not only the hard-earned recipes that have survived the unimaginable atrocities of colonialism but also imparts the knowledge that comes with the foodways that allowed Native peoples to

thrive for thousands of years on this beautiful and diverse land only recently called America—this land that is home to hundreds of tribes with intimate and vast connections to that land. Too often we think of the land only as a backdrop, not as the source of life, and then we exploit it for profit and cut corners for more profit—all at the expense of the health and well-being of the nation's people.

Native American life expectancy is at least five years fewer than that of the rest of all Americans. Too many Native people die of preventable diseases, many diseases that are food-related. When we were dispossessed of our land, we lost many of our sacred foodways. Few understand how the killing of the buffalo went hand in hand with killing Native people and fail to understand how taking our land also meant taking our relationship to the ways we cultivate food, and what food we put into our bodies, and why.

A Feather and a Fork is so much more than a cookbook, and these pages are filled with more than recipes. Crystal Wahpepah is bold in telling us her story, gentle and informative in the way she relays the histories behind the ingredients in these recipes, and generous in the wise way she reminds us that food is medicine and that food can mean home. For those of us with complicated relationships to home, this book is a guide and a beacon. Here we have history, recipe, and knowledge. In short, a vital resource at a time when we need desperately to remember all the ways that we're connected to what we eat and to the land we live on, to the land we owe our lives to, and to all the Indigenous peoples who survived and thrived in order that these foodways could be passed down the generations.

—TOMMY ORANGE

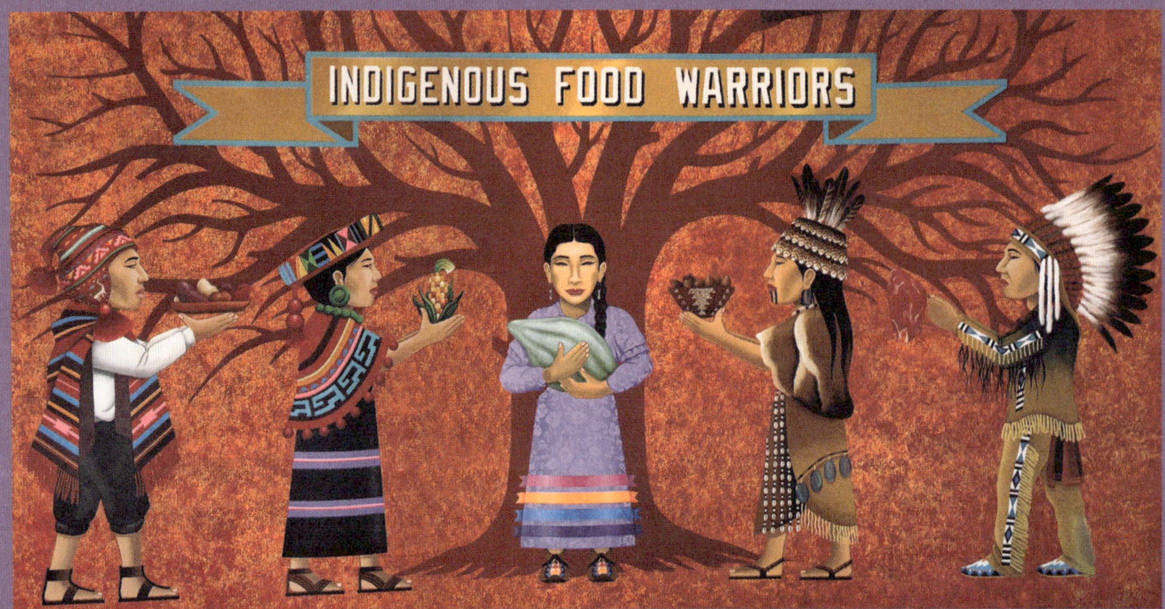
INDIGENOUS FOOD WARRIORS

INTRODUCTION

When most people picture Native Americans, the image they conjure is a relic of the past—stoic warriors and noble Indians in cowboy films. The stereotypical portrayals of Native peoples are grounded in a history of poverty on reservations. Rarely does the broader public acknowledge the modern reality of Native Americans, particularly of those growing up in places like Oakland, California, an inner city far from an idyllic past. The experience of being Native is not defined by the imagery of a vanishing people but by the vibrant, complex lives lived within contemporary society, navigating not only Native American identity but also the challenges of urban life. It is the same with our food.

My restaurant, Wahpepah's Kitchen, sits near the intersection of Avenida de la Fuente and Twelfth Street in Oakland's Fruitvale Transit Village. I was born near here and lived in apartments with my mom and younger sisters off International Boulevard. I attended Lazear Elementary (now Lazear Charter Academy) on Twenty-Ninth Street, and for a time, we lived communally in the American Indian Movement (AIM) Freedom and Survival House at Eighth and Twenty-Seventh Streets. I met my best friend, Yvette, there when she would visit her father, who was close friends with my uncle Bill Wahpepah. Our families knew one another before Yvette and I were even born. We attended what was called survival school, led by my uncle. We learned the multiplication tables and played educational games, like chess. We attended sunrise ceremonies, and the Oakland Fire Department kept extinguishing the fires we lit as part of those ceremonies because they did not understand that the fires were sacred to us. If we were sick, we went to the Native American Health Center. If we were hungry, we received food at the Intertribal Friendship House. Fruitvale—this community—means a lot to me.

From the big arched windows and the outdoor patio at the entrance of Wahpepah's Kitchen, I can see thousands of commuters coming and going daily from the BART station, the one where Oscar Grant III was shot and killed by transit police in 2009. The brilliant blue mural honoring his short life was painted on the west side of the station. Although out of my view, the mural is a reminder to even those passing through that he mattered.

The train tracks are held up by concrete pillars covered in murals of corn, cattails, hibiscus, cactus, and a hummingbird eye—all sacred symbols within the indigenous cultures of the Americas. They represent longevity, sustenance, health, resilience, and strength. Many days local farmers sell freshly picked produce beneath the shade of the tracks to residents and workers in the area and to students who attend Arise High School just above the restaurant.

The walls of Wahpepah's Kitchen too are covered with murals. The columns, painted by New Mexican Diné artist Tony Abeyta, illustrate the centuries-old foundations of my people's food. A wall was designed and painted by a collective of New Mexico–based Native American artists known as NSRGNTS. The artwork pays homage to the precolonial indigenous foods that we serve in the restaurant. On the left, an Incan man carries the potatoes of Peru alongside a Mayan woman offering maize from Mexico. On the right, a Lakota Sioux presents bison as an Ohlone woman bears a basket of acorns. They are all dressed in traditional tribal attire and are walking toward the center, where a Kickapoo woman, who represents my heritage, wears a purple ribbon dress and holds a native squash. The vivid colors evoke the dark red of a South Dakota chokecherry, the deep blue of Ute Mountain corn, the burnished gold of *Zea mays,* and a shade of orange that matches the flesh of a Buffalo Creek squash. Among my staff and me, there are sixteen different tribes represented. On a banner across the top of the mural are the words "Indigenous Food Warriors." That sums up who we are.

The canary yellow shelves of my indigenous food pantry are in full view of our guests and are lined with jars filled with heirloom seeds that have been gifted to me from other tribes—Seneca white corn, blue corn, Lakota popcorn, Pueblo hominy, Pawnee roasted hominy, Kickapoo corn from my Oklahoma family, cracked corn, flint corn, Hubbard squash, and chokecherries from the Lower Butte, the Paiute, and Montana. I want our guests to make the connection between what is on their plates and the bounty of our nation's original foods represented on these shelves. These seeds are very much alive to me, as they each have their own personalities. I talk to them. I pray over them before I plant or cook with them. They are so beautiful, and I have a sacred responsibility to care for them just as I do the people who come to eat.

Many of the neighbors who live in the surrounding community speak Spanish as their first language, but you will hear conversations in Arabic, Farsi, Wolof, and Japanese, among others. We all are striving to make a living, to be seen and heard. And I know how hard it is—to not disappear, to be represented, to wonder where my next meal is coming from, to feel the weight of intergenerational trauma, to lose someone to addiction or preventable disease. No matter what goes on outside my walls, Wahpepah's Kitchen is a place for healing. Food, after all, is medicine. Food is community.

Chími Nu'am
NATIVE CALIFORNIA FOODWAYS
FOR THE CONTEMPORARY KITCHEN

Real Native Romance
Native
Love Jams

Picking Berries
By Hannah Lindoff
with Marigold Lindoff
Illustrated by David Lang
MOVES CAMP
ALTAR

BERRY
Song
CALDECOTT MEDALIST
We Are the Land

Whose Land Do We Walk On?

Oakland is home to some eighteen thousand Native Americans, many of whom descend from the Native Americans relocated to California's East Bay area after World War II, when the U.S. government simultaneously realized that the lands it forcibly removed tribes to during the 1800s held untapped reserves of oil and other minerals and that the cost of maintaining those reservations, however sparse, was too high. So, with the Indian Relocation Acts of 1952 and 1956, the federal government offered the promise of jobs and housing—the American dream—while revoking the status of more than a hundred recognized Native American tribes so that the land on which they had lived and that they had tended was no longer theirs. Oakland—Ohlone land for thousands of years before the arrival of the Spanish—was identified by the Bureau of Indian Affairs as one of seven hubs for American Indian relocation and assimilation into mainstream American life. The only problem was that most of those who relocated arrived with nothing more than a few clothes and a used bus ticket. There was no welcome center.

The mural on the side of the Restore Justice Building at 1419 34th Avenue was painted by Favianna Rodriguez.

Hanging in the halls of the Intertribal Friendship House is a photo of my uncle, Bill Wahpepah, leading a survival school class.

I am an enrolled member of the Kickapoo Tribe of Oklahoma, the first in my family to be born in Oakland. My grandmother was thirteen when she had her first child with Fred Wahpepah. By the time my grandmother was twenty-seven years old, she was a divorced single mother raising six kids on the Sac and Fox reservation in Oklahoma. There was a fourteen-year difference between her first child, my uncle, Fred, and the youngest, my mother, Beverly. My grandmother later married Eugene Makaseah, a friend who grew up on the Kickapoo reservation in McLoud, Oklahoma. Eugene is who I knew as my grandfather. He served in the U.S. Navy and was stationed in Los Angeles. They were relocated to Alameda, just west of Oakland, where my mother and her siblings were raised.

In the novel *There There*, author Tommy Orange wrote, "Look no further than your last name. Follow it back and you might find your line paved with gold, or beset with traps."

"Kickapoo" in the Algonquian language from which the tribe and its bands come means "he who moves here and there." I guess we were destined to wander. But in the Kickapoo language, "Wahpepah" means "entices enemy to ambush."

We Wahpepahs like to stir the pot in our communities.

My grandparents and my mother's older siblings endured the boarding schools that stripped them of their families, their names, their languages, and their dignity—to eradicate the "Indian" inside of them. The abuse and shame that resulted from those experiences coupled with relocation often left them rudderless and seeking solace in substances like alcohol. Uncle Bill struggled with alcohol and relationships before settling into himself in the late 1960s. His younger sister, my aunt Carleta Billy, worked as a clerk with the Bureau of Indian Affairs at the time, and she encouraged him to get involved. He became a leader in the American Indian Movement. In 1975, he was one of the co-founders of the Indigenous Peoples Day Alcatraz Sunrise Gathering when he served as a leader within the International Indian Treaty Council, a body that represented ninety-nine distinct tribes. He led thirty thousand people on a walk from Alcatraz to Washington, D.C., to protest anti-Indian bills working their way through Congress that would further diminish treaty rights. Because of what was dubbed the "Longest Walk," both the Indian Child Welfare Act and the American Indian Religious Freedom Act were signed into law. Aunt Carleta was part of the Indians of All Tribes movement that occupied Alcatraz between 1969 and 1971.

My younger sister, Mercedes, and I were born into this world of activism. Ten years later, another sister was born. We had different fathers and the family moved frequently, often living with other relatives and friends—adopted aunties—as my mother grappled with financial insecurity, mental illness, and alcoholism. By the time I was eleven, we had lived with aunts and uncles throughout the United States and Canada. I can only imagine the conversations among family members: "Who's going to take Beverly's children this time?" But they kept us in the family, no matter whether they could afford to feed us. They put community first, and that community shaped who I am. One aunt taught me how to forage, another how to feed an army with grace.

We lived for a time on the Hoopa Valley Reservation in Northern California between my aunt Teresa Ballenger's home and my aunt Carleta's place. They both let me work alongside them in the kitchen, even when I was little. Aunt Carleta taught me how to make pies and sauces from the berries I picked, and Aunt Teresa taught me everything I know now about hospitality. No one's glass was ever half full—it was always full. At school, I was the new girl in kindergarten, and the kids kept talking about "that Black girl." I looked around to see who they were talking about and realized they were talking about me. I never knew my father, an African American man from the Texas Hill Country, but being mixed race made me different. I was the only African American in our large extended family. Yet, my Native family loved and cared for me. My uncle Bill taught me to be proud of who I am, all the different parts that made me. He gave me books by Alice Walker, a friend of his from the Bay Area, and he taught me to be proud of both my Black and my Native American heritages. Being both Native and Black has given me strength from the ancestors because of where we came from and because of the difficulties we faced through forced displacement.

On those frigid journeys crossing the bay to celebrate the annual gathering on Alcatraz—the clothes, the colors, the passion in the voices calling for recognition, dignity, and basic human rights—my extended family and their friends talked about Indian housing, Indian healthcare, erasure, education, everything. During the meals at La Peña Cultural Center afterward, I always wondered, Where were our foods? Why were our foods never on menus or served in restaurants? How was it that a city like Oakland, home to tens of thousands of Native Americans, had no place that served my grandmother's corn soup?

By then, my grandparents had returned to Shawnee, Oklahoma. When I visited them during the summers, my grandfather would take me berry picking even when I was barely big enough to carry a basket. I considered the sweet, plump, deep purple blackberries as my friends. I listened to them, talked to them, and when things were rough at home, I would escape to the brambles and find my center among the berries. I think I understood even then that food was a gateway to my happiness, to my truest self.

My grandmother and her sister, Aunt Pearl Rolette, taught me how to cut and dry corn in the hot sun for sweet corn soup. That soup is a comfort food to this day. She served it with frybread, which was a treat, even though it was also an emblem of our colonized foodways. At my grandparents' house, we ate frybread or biscuits and gravy three or four times a week. I think even at that young age, though, I already understood there was a big difference between the food that came in a commodity box—white flour, canned vegetables, blocks of bright yellow government cheese—and the food I learned to forage the way the ancestors had. Commodity ingredients represented convenience and industry, meant to make things cheap and easy, but they did not honor Creation.

Those boxes were just another tactic to separate us from ourselves, just like the boarding schools. But for starving Indian families on reservations, who had been displaced from their seeds and their rivers and woods, those boxes held what was sometimes called survival foods. But in the end, those foods are what killed them.

My grandmother, grandfather, Uncle Bill, and other family members all developed diabetes. One aunt's leg was amputated. My grandfather's toe was amputated. My sister died of cancer. So many of these diseases could have been prevented had we found our way to the colorful, beautiful, delicious foods of our ancestors, who call on us to pay attention to our food, how it is grown, and how it is prepared.

For three or four years during childhood, I also lived with Johnella LaRose, a Shoshone-Bannock/Carrizo Native, who met my mother at the AIM House in Oakland. Native people from all over the country lived there and were part of the larger political protest efforts to reclaim their lands, cultures, and religious traditions. They railed against the Bureau of Indian Affairs and the entrenched policies that led to high unemployment, slum living conditions, chronic physical and mental illnesses, and persistent poverty among rural and urban Native Americans. The AIM House offered a communal experience, and I was often in the kitchen right beside Johnella, my adopted auntie, cooking for thirty kids and as many adults a night. I was seven years old.

So, it was only natural that I would grow up to feed my community.

My Auntie Johnella LaRose is one of the co-founders of the Segorea Te' Land Trust, an organization that helped me get started in catering.

The Birth of a Food Warrior

First, though, I went to the American Indian College in Phoenix to study business. I had never seen someone who looked like me lead a restaurant—at least not until Loretta Barrett Oden, a Citizen Potawatomi, opened the Corn Dance Café in Santa Fe, New Mexico, in 1993. All along, I worked in restaurants, both in the back and front of house to make ends meet, even after I married a man I grew up with and gave birth to three daughters. For fourteen years, my husband and I lived in Shawnee, Oklahoma, near my mother, sister, and cousins, who all had returned to the Kickapoo tribal lands.

The Kickapoo can be insular people. One article I read said that anthropologists consider the Kickapoo the least assimilated tribe among the nation's 574 federally recognized tribes. We are protective because of all that was stolen from us, all that we had to hide to remain Kickapoo. But after fourteen years away and with a disintegrating marriage, I missed Oakland, and I wanted to go to culinary school.

My daughters stayed in Oklahoma with their father to finish school, and I traveled back and forth until they all moved back to Oakland. I enrolled at Le Cordon Bleu in San Francisco from 2008 to 2010, but I did not graduate because I was trying to balance being a full-time student and a mother, and I realized the school could never teach me what I had to learn. I wanted the skills—you know, the ones steeped in French tradition—but there was so much competition. Everyone knew what kind of chef they wanted to be, and they wanted to be the executive chef not for the love of the food but for the potential for fame. I stood out, the other once again, as the one who wanted to bring Native American cuisine to restaurant tables so that we could celebrate a rich and long heritage of honoring the land and waters and what they provided beyond sustenance. I wanted to let the purest, simplest, freshest ingredients—like berries and blue corn—sing together.

When I scoured the Oakland library for cookbooks by people like me, I couldn't find any until I stumbled on Lois Ellen Frank's *Native American Cooking*. It was a revelation because I finally had found a book that spoke my language of heirloom, indigenous ingredients. That book and a few others I found inspired me to take the leap to start Wahpepah's Kitchen, first as a side hustle to make ends meet, then as a catering business in 2010, cooking out of a commercial kitchen until I could get established.

One of my first real catering jobs was for the Native American Health Center. Martin Waukazoo and Katherine Lewis asked me to cater for four hundred people at the Gathering of the Lodges event that focused on sobriety and well-being. I tapped friends from culinary school to help, and we could see as people were eating the corn soup and cornbread that they felt something healing was happening. I saw that same sense of healing happen all across the community as people reconnected with their foods, even when businesses in Silicon Valley, such as Google and Facebook, started to call. I used every event to talk about indigenous foodways, and I cooked with as many ingredients by Native growers and producers as I could find. I grew close to the educators and ethnobotanists at The Cultural Conservancy, a Native-led, Bay Area nonprofit that, among many things, grows beans, corns, squash, berries, grains, lettuces, stone fruits, and herbs from indigenous seeds gathered and gifted from Native communities. We still grow produce for the restaurant at The Cultural Conservancy farm at Heron Shadow.

Bonney Hartley, a member of the Stockbridge-Munsee Mohican Nation, was the director of community services at the Native American Health Center during that time, and she heard about a business incubation program called La Cocina. In 2010, Native American Health offered to sponsor me for the program so that I could connect with mentors—like Bill Dickenson, who worked for five-star restaurants—and develop the dishes and business that would ultimately become Wahpepah's Kitchen. The restaurant grew from a catering business to periodic pop-ups around Oakland and in Fruitvale, where we introduced more people to the striking beauty and pure tastes of Native American dishes, like blackberry chia pudding and smoked salmon and hibiscus tostadas.

The Covid-19 pandemic hit both Native communities and the restaurant industry hard. Catering orders dried up, and the commercial kitchen I had been using in downtown Oakland for years closed. Palestinian-Syrian chef and community activist Reem Assil invited me to host a pop-up dinner at her bakery in the Fruitvale Transit Village in 2020. When she decided to shutter her bakery the following year, Reem asked if I wanted to take over the space. My community surrounded me with support—emotional, spiritual, financial—and in November 2021, Wahpepah's Kitchen opened its doors. It is Oakland's first female Indigenous–owned restaurant.

The first day the restaurant was open, an older man came in and ordered the blue corn cake. As he ate, he began to cry. He had not been home to his reservation since he was eighteen years old, he said, and eating these foods was like leading him home. When he thanked me, I knew—in spite of all my fears of taking on the responsibility of a brick-and-mortar space—that I was on the right road.

> **Everywhere I go, I say the same thing. It is traumatizing for people who are connected to the land to see the land being abused. It is like seeing a member of your family beaten, bruised, and broken. By reconnecting to these first foods, we are healing not only our broken bodies but transforming the generational trauma into strength and regenerating the earth. By sharing our foods, we are helping our neighbors heal as well. This is the reason I have written *A Feather and a Fork*.**

Not long ago, some talented students from East Oakland's Fremont High School, many of them Indigenous, built garden boxes for the restaurant as part of their arts and culture program. They returned in the rain and helped plant the boxes with edible flowers that also brought greenery and beauty to Fruitvale Village. Afterward, we shared acorn cookies and huckleberry limeade and talked about food sovereignty in our community and what it means to have true access to our foods. When they left the restaurant that day, I prayed that they walked more gently on the land and will, in turn, take better care of it.

Wahpepah's
Kitchen
A HOPITI KE NO

OAKLAND
NATIVE
LAND
GP 24

ABOUT THIS BOOK

A ho pi ti ke no. Welcome.

These words are written on the board above the counter as guests come into Wahpepah's Kitchen. They extend to all of you who hold this book in your hands. Food and community have always been my spiritual center. With this book, I am inviting you into a way of thinking about the food you cook for yourself and your family that is rooted in the oldest traditions of my people and of this land we now share. These traditions represent the key to not only our physical, mental, and spiritual health but also to the health of our planet. What we grow, how we grow it, and how we distribute the food to our communities can change how we live with one another and begin to solve so many of the problems that separate us from one another and ourselves.

According to the National Institutes of Health, nearly three-quarters of Americans are overweight or obese, with more than 42 percent falling into the obese category. For non-Hispanic American Indian/Alaska Natives, the situation is worse: The Office of Minority Health reports that Native American students in grades 9 to 12 were 30 percent more likely to be obese, and adults were 40 percent more likely to be obese than their non-Hispanic white peers. Heart disease, diabetes, and hypertension are, largely, food-related illnesses. I have lost so many loved ones to these diseases, and my guess is, you have too. The irony is that two-plus centuries of policies by the very same government that compiled these devastating statistics have allowed for the proliferation of these preventable and curable diseases, as well as healthcare inequities, addiction, and food deserts, where people are bereft of access to fresh produce, not to mention green spaces to breathe in fresh air and walk in nature, hear the rush of a creek over rock, pluck and enjoy the taste of a sun-warmed blackberry from a wild bramble. We have lost our relationship with Turtle Island, the name many Indigenous groups call this land, and the food we put into our bodies. This loss plays out in a kind of grief we have not yet worked through.

Indigenous communities are actively endeavoring to decolonize nutrition and reclaim sovereignty over their traditional foodways through growing again from their heirloom seeds according to native values and contemporary ecological knowledge. I believe this is the beginning of putting us into the right relationship with our food once again. Studies have shown that traditional crops' nutritional value is higher than comparable commercial crops, in which soils have been stripped of their vital salutary components through monocultural growing practices, overuse of synthetic pesticides, and genetic modification. I am hopeful that I and my fellow Indigenous food warriors—folks like chef Sean Sherman, husband-and-wife farmers and ethnobotanists Luke (Ahán Heȟáka Sápa) Black Elk and Linda

Black Elk, educator Melissa Nelson and the farmers at The Cultural Conservancy, and the producers at the *Native Seed Pod* podcast, among so many others—deliver a message that you hear and not only embrace but also evangelize.

But it is not enough to simply have access to native ingredients. We have to know their history, their many uses, and how to cook with them. The recipes that follow are modern interpretations of a precolonial Native American diet, where I use the freshest, most local ingredients I can find produced with the least amount of intervention or modification by commercial agricultural practices. I rely mostly on fruits and vegetables grown or foraged through traditional indigenous practices, and I use very little wheat or dairy. I use no pork but do include the leanest proteins from wild game, such as deer and turkey, and Native-produced bison, rabbit, and seafood. Sea salt is used throughout for seasoning, but I prefer aromatics and herbs for flavor. I source products from Indigenous growers who use sustainable, traditional methods, not only to walk the walk but also to help build Native American economies. Near the end of this book, on page 291, you will find a list of some of the producers from whom I source.

The chapters are organized by types of ingredients, beginning with the foundation of Native American cuisine—beans, corn, and squash. The subsequent recipes are uncomplicated but are filled with the flavor and personality of the specific ingredients and are accompanied by indigenous wisdom regarding the health benefits of ingredients and how that intuitive knowledge is backed by science. I encourage you to use seasonal ingredients grown by local farmers and Native American producers, and to take foraging classes to seek out wild lettuces, mushrooms, and fruits so that you can taste the richness of unprocessed food, perhaps for the first time. Make substitutions where necessary. If you do not have pure maple sugar or syrup on hand, use raw honey gathered locally or small-batch agave syrup, true molasses, or sorghum—harvested with care for the earth. The darker the syrup or molasses, the denser the nutrients.

More than anything, I want the idea of Native American food to *not* be an anomaly. These bright, healthy, sustainable foods and foodways are the truly original American diet, grown naturally and made here for millennia. We should not be strangers to these foods, but in community with them.

WHAT IS TURTLE ISLAND?

Among many of the tribes that descend from the Anishinaabe, the original peoples of the Great Lakes region, such as the Ojibwe, Algonquin, and Oji-Cree, the turtle represents the creation story of the earth, supporting life itself. When the world was covered in water by a great flood, as the myth goes, mud was placed on a giant turtle's back to carry the land that is now known as North America. Calling this land Turtle Island is an act of resistance, an effort to reclaim the deep spiritual connection Native Americans have to Mother Earth, a cherished loved one.

ENTERING
KICKAPOO
NATION

KICKAPOO GLOSSARY

It is important to me that the restaurant, the events we cater, and my advocacy work with different organizations become opportunities to not only teach about Native American foods but also to take steps toward healing the psychological and emotional wounds that have been carried from one generation to the next. Reclaiming our native foods is step one toward rebuilding our strength, eradicating nutrition-based diseases, and restoring our vitality.

Reclaiming our voice is second. At Wahpepah's Kitchen, every seasonal dish's name is listed on the menu with both its Kiikaapoa and English translations. I have done the same with the recipes in this cookbook so that you can see and sound out the lilting musicality of my tribe's native tongue, a language, like so many other Native American customs and traditions, that almost was lost forever. Each tribal nation speaks a distinct language and holds unique ceremonies, and that is why it is so important to remember and to pass along the culture.

Beginning in the late 1800s, the U.S. government began to systematically take Native American children around the age of five from their families and send them to Native American boarding schools, which were run like military academies to essentially erase anything "Indian." Christian missionaries, Bureau of Indian Affairs instructors, and bureau administrators stripped generations of Native Americans like my grandparents, aunts, and uncles of their given names, cut their hair, punished them for speaking their own languages, humiliated them for wanting to practice their ceremonies—all under the U.S. Department of the Interior's 1883 Code of Indian Offenses and in the guise of assimilating the people who had inhabited this land for millennia into the colonizers' ways of life. Not until Congress passed the American Indian Religious Freedom Act in 1978 did Native Americans have the right to freely "believe, express, and exercise the traditional religions of the American Indian, Eskimo, Aleut, and Native Hawaiians" through ceremonies and spiritual rites.

Because of these restrictions that were meant to shame, many indigenous languages and cultural traditions remained hidden, and were practiced in secret. The elders like my aunts Ruth and Carleta continued to keep and tell the stories and to pass them down. My oldest daughter, Rosario (Big Valley Pomo and Kickapoo), is the language keeper for our family and the benefactor of an elder within the Kickapoo Tribe of Oklahoma, who has helped identify the words and names of the ingredients so that the Wahpepah's Kitchen menu honors the ancestors' memories, sacrifices, and perseverance. By sharing these words, we keep the language alive and show our gratitude for all who came before.

KIIKAAPOA	ENGLISH
Aamenookamiiki	Spring
Aaskipakiyaaki	Green
Aapikooni	Squash
Apetei	Warm
Ceyaka (Lakota)	Mint tea
Chaakaneti	Chocolate
Chaakisii Memeethaki	Fish of all kinds
Chaakisii Pahkwesikani	Sweet breads and cakes of all kinds
Chipaeesiihooni	Mushroom
Chipitiini	Hot chili pepper
Ihskopahaakani	Salt
Ihskopihpeniiya	Sweet potato
Katoowakimina	Chokecherry
Kaskinwiihi	Pumpkin
Keetahteehi	Frybread
Kohkisaani	Cookies
Maakomisi	Sumac
Mahskochiithaki	Beans
Manoomini	Wild rice
Meekateethichik Miinaki	Blackberries
Mehtekomini	Acorn
Mehsweeha	Rabbit
Mehskopwaakaa	Prickly Pear
Mekohi Ithakahaakanaapowi	Salsa
Menetheehi	Island
Mesiimina	Apple
Meskwaaki Eteeteeki	Pomegranate
Methiikwaki	Corn
Miikieni Okweeminaki	Amaranth
Miinaki	Berries, such as blueberries, raspberries, cranberries, and huckleberries
Miinekaanani	Seeds, such as quinoa
Misiikwaa	Bison
Myaanaweekwaapowi	Catfish
Neowi	Number three (3)
Nepi	Water, river
Nepoopii	Stew or soup
Ochiikaapowi	Tea
Ohpeniyeeki	Potatoes
Oopikai	Ribs
Otaatopakooni	Salad/leaves/salad
Otaatopakwi	Sage/leave
Oteehiminani	Strawberry
Ototeemetiaki	Sisters
Pahteewi	To smoke or smoked
Pakaana	Pecan
Pakaanani	Nuts
Peesekithi'a	Deer, venison
Peeskipaateeki	Blue
Peeskoneiihi	Flowers
Pemi	Oil
Peneewa	Turkey
Piipihskiihi	Breads, like cornbreads
Saakahneehaki	Onions
Sekwaakwa	Cedar
Siisiipe'a	Duck
Taakohaki	Taco
Takwahaani	Hominy
Tanokootenwi	Floating
Thiithapaakwamisi	Maple and other sweeteners, such as agave syrup and honey
Wiiyaathi	Meat

1

THE THREE SISTERS

Neowi Ototeemetiaki

The rise of corporate agriculture, or Big Ag, around the world relies on singular and often genetically modified monocultures plus lots of chemicals and soil additives to produce massive crop yields. And while this approach may economically make sense on paper to feed multitudes at the lowest price point possible in this day and age, it has harmed our physical health, emotional well-being, and the very Creation that supports life. This truth applies not just to Indigenous peoples, who have been harmed by the federal commodified foods program, but to all of us who have come to rely on cheap and easy processed foods to feed our families. We no longer get the nutrients we need from our food and spend lots of money on supplementing our diets. We develop chronic diseases that can be avoided and even cured through better eating habits. Our sense of taste betrays us. Until you taste a wild onion still warm from the sun, you have no idea how Creator meant an onion to taste, how Creator made it for your joy, sustenance, and health.

Pre-Columbian-era Native American societies understood both intuitively and through hundreds of years of trial and error how to live with the land and the elements. They abided organic, regenerative agricultural practices long before those concepts became labels on supermarket produce or expensive college classes. The early Mississippian culture along the Mississippi and Tennessee River Valleys spawned a vast maize-based agrarian network from what is now the Midwest and throughout the southeastern United States. The Iroquois and Cherokee tribes that grew from these traditions planted corn, beans, and squash together, because of how the three crops nurtured one another and the soil like family—that is why they are called the Three Sisters. Beans pulled nitrogen from the air and fed it to the dirt. Squash spread their leaves as ground cover to tamp down weeds so that the corn could shoot high, reaching for the sun. The Three Sisters form the foundation of an indigenous diet and have become legend among many different tribes (see the Kickapoo Legend of the Three Sisters on page 50). They signify strength by growing together—a lesson for us all.

THE THREE SISTERS

Neowi Ototeemetiaki

BEANS

Mahskochiithaki

CORN

Methiikwaki

SQUASH
Aapikooni

THREE SISTERS VEGGIE BOWL

Neowi Ototeemetiaki Otaatopakooni

SERVES 4 This recipe showcases one of my signature dishes that made the leap from my home kitchen to the catering table and then to Wahpepah's Kitchen. I spent years playing with the combination of ingredients, sometimes using red or wild rice, adding and subtracting fruits, nuts, and seeds based on what was in season. No matter the variations, the bowl always is anchored by tepary beans, which are a hearty, drought-resistant runner indigenous to the southwestern deserts that dates back to the pre-Columbian era; Buffalo Creek squash, a sweet, deep orange heirloom varietal from the Great Lakes region; and rustic dried hominy corn from either the Pueblo or the Pawnee. Because there are multiple ingredients and steps to craft this healthy and filling bowl, I often make it at home when I have some leftover quinoa and kale.

FOR THE BEANS

1 cup white tepary beans

1 teaspoon sea salt

FOR THE SQUASH

1 small (3 to 5 pounds) Buffalo Creek squash, peeled, seeded, and cubed

2 teaspoons olive oil

1 teaspoon sea salt

½ teaspoon freshly ground black pepper

FOR THE CRACKED CORN

½ cup dried yellow or white hominy

1 teaspoon sea salt

FOR THE QUINOA

1 cup tricolor quinoa

½ teaspoon sea salt

To make the beans

▶ Rinse and sort the tepary beans and soak them in water to cover for 1 hour prior to cooking. Drain the beans well, then fill a large saucepan with 8 cups water, the salt, and beans. Bring the water to a boil over high heat, then reduce the heat to low. Cover and simmer the beans for about 2 hours, until tender. While the beans cook, prepare the other ingredients.

▶ Once the beans are done, drain them through a sieve or colander, and cool.

To roast the squash

▶ Preheat the oven to 350°F.

▶ Toss the cubed squash in the oil, salt, and pepper in a bowl, then spread in a single layer on a baking sheet or in a roasting pan. Roast the squash for 15 to 20 minutes, until tender and lightly browned.

To cook the cracked corn

▶ Bring the dried hominy, salt, and 4 cups water to a boil in a large saucepan over high heat. Reduce the heat to low, cover, and simmer the hominy for 45 minutes, or until tender. Drain through a sieve or colander, and cool.

Continued

FOR THE KALE

1 pound kale

2 teaspoons olive oil

1 teaspoon sea salt

FOR THE BOWL

1 large red onion, chopped

1 cup fresh blueberries and raspberries

1 cup raw sunflower seeds

1 cup chopped raw walnuts

1 tablespoon puffed amaranth, for garnish

½ cup Maple Oil (recipe follows), for serving

½ cup Chili Oil (recipe follows), for serving

To make the quinoa

▶ Rinse the quinoa in a fine-mesh sieve under cold running water for at least 30 seconds. Drain well.

▶ Bring the quinoa, salt, and 2 cups water to a boil in a medium saucepan over high heat. Reduce the heat to low and let the quinoa simmer for 15 to 20 minutes, until all the water is absorbed. Remove the pan from the heat, cover, and let the quinoa rest for 5 minutes.

▶ Fluff the quinoa with a fork before serving.

To braise the kale

▶ Rinse and pat dry the kale. Remove the stems and coarsely chop the leaves.

▶ Heat the oil in a large deep-sided skillet over medium-high heat. Toss the kale in the skillet for about 2 minutes, until it begins to slightly wilt. Stir in the salt.

To assemble the bowls

▶ Divide the beans, squash, cracked corn, quinoa, kale, onions, blueberries, sunflower seeds, and walnuts equally among 4 large bowls. Serve with a sprinkling of puffed amaranth and sides of maple oil and chili oil to toss with the ingredients.

Notes

Sweet corn can substitute for dried hominy. Hubbard or butternut squash are flavorful substitutes for the Buffalo Creek squash.

Feel free to alternate ingredients according to what is in season. The recipe here, with the blueberries, is the late-spring version. In early spring, use strawberries. For summer, add blackberries or peaches. For fall and winter, serve warm, as in the variation on page 48, and use marinated hibiscus flowers and pomegranate seeds for health, color, and texture.

MAPLE OIL

MAKES 2 CUPS

1 cup pure maple syrup

1 cup olive oil

¼ teaspoon sea salt

▶ Whisk the maple syrup, oil, and salt in a medium saucepan over low heat until the salt dissolves. Remove the saucepan from the heat and allow it to cool.

▶ Transfer the oil to an airtight container and store it at room temperature for up to 2 weeks or in the refrigerator for up to 6 months.

GOOD MEDICINE

I prefer pure indigenous maple syrups, such as Spirit Lake Native Farms, which is produced on the Fond du Lac Reservation in Minnesota; the Passamaquoddy tribe's 100 percent pure Grade A amber maple syrup from Maine; and the Grade A dark amber by Native Wise. See the Resources on page 291.

Food scientists have found that pure maple syrup is loaded with twenty-four natural antioxidants, those acids, polyphenols, and flavonoids that reduce inflammation throughout the body and aid digestion. Maple syrup is chock-full of minerals such as zinc, manganese, potassium, and calcium, which are beneficial on a cellular level. And while pure maple syrup does spike insulin levels, it has a much lower score on the glycemic index than processed white sugar and corn syrup because it is absorbed more slowly through the liver. So, it must be used in small amounts.

Just like raw honey, maple syrup can be applied directly to the skin to soothe dry red patches and even the inflammation of blemishes. Mixed into a yogurt-and-oat face mask, it can relieve the redness from rosacea while also moisturizing.

CHILI OIL

MAKES 2 CUPS

1 cup grapeseed oil

¼ cup olive oil

½ cup finely chopped yellow onion

1 cinnamon stick

1 star anise

1 chile de arbol (bird's beak chili)

1 New Mexican chili

1 garlic clove, finely chopped

1 tablespoon whole black peppercorns

1 tablespoon crushed red pepper flakes

1 teaspoon chile de arbol powder

¼ teaspoon granulated onion

½ teaspoon granulated garlic

½ teaspoon pure maple syrup

¼ teaspoon sea salt

1 drop distilled white vinegar

▸ Combine all the ingredients in a medium saucepan over medium-low heat. Bring the mixture to a gentle boil, reduce the heat to low, and simmer for 10 minutes. Remove the pan from the heat and allow the mixture to cool.

▸ Strain the chili oil through a fine-mesh strainer into a sealable glass container. Keep at room temperature for up to 3 weeks or in the refrigerator for up to 6 months.

TIP

Throughout the recipes, you will see maple, chili, and maple-chili oils as ingredients. To get the sweet heat of the Maple-Chili Oil, combine the ingredients from the Maple Oil (page 45) and the Chili Oil recipes and cook according to the chili oil instructions.

WARM THREE SISTERS SALAD WITH CRANBERRIES

Apetei Neowi Ototeemetiaki Otaatopakooni

SERVES 4 Spring and early summer in Northern California can be chilling to the bone while the rest of the country is blooming with color and folks are shedding their layers to warm their skin in the sun. I am usually bundled in fleece pullovers and craving warmth and comfort foods, like this toasty, aromatic adaption of the Three Sisters Veggie Bowl (page 43). There is a bit of seesaw between sweet and savory with the pungent garlic and peppery arugula and the intensity of dried cranberries. This salad is full of vivid colors. I just love the marbled cranberry beans that turn a pale mauve color when cooked, like pink granite or pipestone. While this recipe calls for arugula or mixed greens because those are more readily available, foraged dandelion greens and other wild lettuces offer that same sharp note.

2 cups red cranberry beans

1 teaspoon sea salt

2 cups cubed butternut squash

5 whole garlic cloves

2 sprigs of fresh rosemary

½ cup olive oil

¼ teaspoon freshly ground black pepper

1 cup cooked hominy (see page 43)

1 small red onion, diced

2 cups dried cranberries

1 pound arugula or mixed greens

¼ cup Maple-Chili Oil (see Tip, page 46)

Note

Feel free to use leftover cooked squash or pumpkin and substitute a 15.5-ounce can of white or yellow hominy, drained, in this recipe.

▸ Rinse and sort the cranberry beans and soak them in water to cover for 1 hour prior to cooking. Drain the beans well, then fill a large saucepan with 8 cups water, ½ teaspoon salt, and beans. Bring the water to a boil over high heat, then reduce the heat to low. Cover and simmer the beans for about 2 hours, until tender. While the beans cook, you can prepare the other ingredients.

▸ Preheat the oven to 350°F.

▸ Toss the cubed squash, garlic, rosemary sprigs, oil, the remaining ½ teaspoon salt, and pepper in a bowl, then spread in a single layer on a baking sheet or in a roasting pan. Roast for 15 to 20 minutes, until the squash is tender and lightly browned.

▸ Remove the leaves from the rosemary sprigs and sprinkle over the squash. Mash the garlic into a soft paste.

▸ Drain the cooked beans. While the beans and squash are still warm, toss the beans, squash, garlic paste, hominy, onion, cranberries, arugula, and maple-chili oil together in a large bowl. The arugula will wilt slightly. Taste and adjust the salt and pepper to your liking.

▸ Divide the salad among 4 medium bowls and cozy up for a healthy lunch or dinner.

GOOD MEDICINE

Bog cranberries (*Vaccinium oxycoccos*) are super high in vitamin C. Although they are antioxidant powerhouses that support overall health, they are especially helpful to the bladder and kidneys. Because cranberries have such a short fall harvest, freeze fresh ones to use throughout the year to make homemade juices and sauces, or dehydrate them to throw into cereals and salads.

KICKAPOO LEGEND OF THE THREE SISTERS

My cousin Kathy Wahpepah recently shared with me the story her father told her about the Kickapoo legend of the Three Sisters. This is our story about corn, beans, and squash—I'll try to tell it as best as I can.

▲▲▲

It begins in a time when there was a great struggle among our people. They were running out of food, and the place where they were living could no longer support all the people. The hunters had to go farther and farther from their homes to find food. It was so difficult that the elders were giving away their food so that the children didn't have to starve. It was concerning for the people in the village because they were all one big family. They tried to take care of one another.

And in that village were a mother and her son. They could hear the children crying from hunger. They saw their elders struggling. Mother knew the hunters would not be back soon, as they had to travel far from the village to get the food that they would all need to live. The best thing that they could do was pray.

Every night they prayed. They made their offerings of tobacco so that Creator would hear them. They did this every night until one morning, the mother went to find her son and he was not there. She was worried because she thought, maybe, he had gone with the hunters, but he was too young. All day as she went about her work, she kept her eye on the horizon, looking for her son to return from the direction he might have gone. When he did not return, she prayed for him to be safe, because praying was the only thing she knew to do.

She had a fitful sleep that night. The next morning, she rose early and again watched the horizon for her son to return. She saw a tiny speck, something that caught her attention. As the day went on, the speck grew bigger, as if someone were coming toward her. She fixed that spot in her vision and watched it all day long. For sure, that spot in the distance started to get bigger and bigger. Certainly, someone was coming toward the village, and she hoped it was her son.

As she continued to watch, the spot on the horizon continued to grow bigger and bigger. She thought she saw broad shoulders and hair sticking up the way his hair always did. It looked like a person, and she thought she could see feet. She convinced herself, "Yes, yes! I think that is my son."

The figure seemed to be growing bigger and getting closer to her. She was certain it was her son, so she began to walk toward him. Then she ran. Finally, she arrived right where she had seen this figure on the horizon. But she did not find her son. Instead, she saw it was a plant—a very tall plant with a

tassel on the top. The leaves were big and broad, arched out from the stalk, and must have been what she thought were the shoulders. A second plant with pods wound around the stalk, making it appear fuller, to look more like a person. She saw then that there was a third plant around the bottom. Among the big broad leaves was a long fruit. The mother stood back and realized that this was her son. He had given himself so that the people would have food.

And so, we treasure these three foods—corn, beans, and squash—because we recognize them for what they are: a relative of ours. And we care for them in the same way we would care for someone we love, and we acknowledge this boy who was too young to become a warrior, too young to become a hunter, but became what fed our people from that day on.

THREE SISTERS QUINOA

Neowi Ototeemetiaki Miinekaanani

SERVES 4 Archaeological research shows that thousands of years before the Incas built a civilization in Peru, the Andean Indigenous peoples cultivated quinoa. It is a tall, bushy ancient self-pollinating grain that comes in red, white, green, purple, and black varieties, and its seeds pack a high-fiber, high-protein punch. A little bit will fill you and keep you energized for hours. When roasting squash and making beans for the previous recipes, make a little extra to throw into this quick, savory side or main dish, which takes only 10 to 20 minutes to make with a little forethought.

2 cups tricolored quinoa

1 cup roasted butternut squash (see page 49)

½ cup cooked black, cranberry, or white tepary beans (see page 43)

½ cup cooked corn kernels

1 tablespoon pure maple syrup

2 wild green onions (scallions), white and green parts thinly sliced, for garnish

▸ Bring 3 cups water to boil in a medium saucepan over high heat.

▸ While the water is coming to a boil, soak the quinoa in a large fine-mesh sieve set in a bowl of cold water for 2 to 3 minutes.

▸ Strain the quinoa and stir it into the boiling water. Reduce the heat to low and cook, covered, for about 15 minutes, until the water is absorbed and the quinoa is fluffy.

▸ Fold in the squash, beans, corn, and maple syrup until well distributed. Divide evenly among 4 plates, garnish with the wild green onions, and serve.

THREE SISTERS STEW WITH VENISON

Neowi Ototeemetiaki Peesekithi'a Nepoopii

SERVES 4 TO 6 The Three Sisters are adaptable to all seasons and styles of cooking, especially slow-cooked stews. One-pot cookery is an economical way of extending the life of ingredients, tenderizing tough game, layering flavors, and feeding large numbers of people with something sustaining and energizing. I serve most stews and soups with a square of Sweet Blue Cornbread (page 81) for dipping or crumbling as an added bit of texture and heartiness.

1 cup black or white tepary beans

2 tablespoons vegetable oil

1 pound venison stew meat

4 cups cubed butternut squash

1 cup dried white hominy

3 garlic cloves

6 cups Vegetable Stock (page 97)

1 sprig of fresh rosemary

1 teaspoon sea salt

½ teaspoon freshly ground black pepper

▶ Rinse and sort the tepary beans and soak them in water to cover for 1 hour prior to cooking.

▶ Heat the oil in a large stockpot over medium heat. Add the stew meat and brown for 2 to 3 minutes per side, until it is golden brown all over. Remove the stew meat and set it aside.

▶ Add the squash, hominy, and garlic to the same pot and cook, stirring occasionally, for 5 to 7 minutes, until just beginning to get tender and golden. Drain the beans, then return the stew meat and the beans to the pot and pour the vegetable stock over the meat and vegetables. Toss in the rosemary, then raise the heat to high and bring the stew to a boil.

▶ Reduce the heat to medium-low and cook the stew for about 1 hour, until the beans are nice and tender and the venison has cooked through. Serve hot with a side of cornbread.

▶ Store any leftover stew in an airtight container in the refrigerator for up to 4 days.

THE ROAD TO LUCK

When I began catering nearly twenty-five years ago, I never imagined I would get the chance to cook for the legendary singer-songwriter Willie Nelson, whose mother was three-quarters Cherokee. But in 2023, a request came from Michel Nischan, the co-founder and chairman of Wholesome Wave, a national nonprofit that has increased access to healthy fruits and vegetables for low-income Americans by doubling Supplemental Nutrition Assistance Program (SNAP) benefits and using produce as medicine to combat nutritional insecurity and food-related diseases.

Wholesome Wave is one of the three nonprofit organizations, including Farm Aid and the Texas Food and Wine Alliance in Austin, that are beneficiaries of the annual Potluck, a truly special meal served every March on the eve of the Luck Reunion, an all-day music festival on Nelson's ranch in the hills above Spicewood, Texas. The feast for about three hundred people serves as a fundraiser for the Luck Family Foundation and its goals of preserving sustainable and accessible foodways, family farms, and the American Roots legacy.

Each year the meal centers on a theme. In 2023, the foundation selected the Three Sisters, and I was invited as one of three Native American female chefs to contribute to the four-course meal. I made my family's Kickapoo Chili (page 206) in a huge cast-iron pot over an open flame and served it with a slice of Sweet Blue Cornbread (page 81). I followed that with a chokecherry-rubbed Bison Roast slow-smoked over low heat outdoors. For dessert, I developed a light cake made from three ingredients I had used in the other dishes—Buffalo Creek squash, Ramona Farms' white tepary beans, and roasted corn.

THREE SISTERS CAKE

Neowi Ototeemetiaki Chaakisii Pahkwesikani

SERVES 8 This light and slightly sweet dessert sits at the intersection of cornbread and tea cake in terms of texture. It is ideal for a small gathering and affords a bit of that "funfetti" appeal with the golden hints of corn and squash in the batter. The maple cream acts like an icing without overpowering the subtle flavors. I hope baking this cake brings you as much "Luck" as it did me.

1½ cups all-purpose flour

1 cup white cornmeal

2 tablespoons baking powder

1 teaspoon sea salt

1 cup (2 sticks) unsalted butter, at room temperature

½ cup pure maple sugar (see Resources, page 291)

3 large duck eggs

1 teaspoon Mexican vanilla extract

½ cup cooked white tepary beans (see page 43), puréed into a loose, smooth slurry

½ cup cooked small-kernel corn (cut from the cob)

¼ cup cooked finely diced butternut squash

Maple Cream (page 58), for serving

Note

This recipe calls for duck eggs, but if you do not have access to duck eggs, substitute 2 large chicken eggs for each duck egg.

▸ Preheat the oven to 375°F. Butter a 9-inch round baking pan. Line the baking pan with parchment paper.

▸ Stir together the flour, cornmeal, baking powder, and salt in a large bowl.

▸ Cream the butter and maple sugar in the bowl of a stand mixer fitted with the paddle attachment on medium-high speed for 3 to 5 minutes, until the butter and sugar are light yellow and fluffy. Reduce the mixer speed to low and add the eggs, one at a time, beating until completely blended.

▸ Add the vanilla, then raise the mixer speed to medium-low. Beat in the flour mixture, scraping down the sides of the bowl periodically to make sure all of it is incorporated, 2 to 3 minutes.

▸ Reduce the mixer speed to its lowest setting and mix in the bean purée. Turn off the mixer and scrape the paddle, then gently fold in the corn and squash by hand.

▸ Pour the batter into the prepared pan. Bake the cake for 15 to 25 minutes, until the top is golden brown and the edges have pulled away from the pan. Allow the cake to cool in the pan for at least 10 minutes, then turn it out onto a wire rack to cool completely.

▸ Cut the cake into 8 slices and drizzle with the maple cream just before serving.

WHY DUCK EGGS?

Native Americans did not raise chickens, nor did the yard birds run wild throughout the Americas until well after Columbus, so chicken eggs never factored into the indigenous diet. Duck eggs, on the other hand, were available in the wild, near ponds, rivers, and lakes, in the fringes of reeds and cattails, in woodland underbrush, and sometimes in trees. Duck eggs are bigger in size and volume than chicken eggs, and their yolks are about twice the size of those of chickens—meaning more protein, fat, and flavor per ounce.

MAPLE CREAM

MAKES 4 CUPS Instead of sweetened whipped cream or a cloying frosting as a topper or finish to a square of Three Sisters Cake (page 56) or Blue Corn Cupcakes (page 104), I turn to this simple maple cream for a delicate hint of caramel with a soft note of brown sugar. All that is required is pure maple syrup, patience, and some sweat equity to create this light and luscious confection. You will know it is ready once the color has lightened and the texture is thick but spreadable.

4 cups pure maple syrup

- Pour the maple syrup into a large saucepan over medium-high heat and heat it to 235°F on a candy/deep-fry thermometer without stirring.
- Once the maple syrup is bubbling and has reached 235°F, remove the pan from the heat and set it in a large metal bowl filled with ice. The ice bath will bring the syrup's temperature down quickly. Once it drops to 100°F, stir the syrup, not vigorously but continuously for 15 to 20 minutes, until the syrup grows lighter in color, glossy, and creamy, like the consistency of softened butter.
- Transfer to an airtight container and store in the refrigerator for up to 6 months.

A TOUCH OF SWEETNESS

There is no direct translation in the Kickapoo language for maple syrup, but in the Sac and Fox language, which is similar because it is part of the same Algonquian linguistic tradition, the word is "menêshishi."

The importance of menêshishi to Native American foodways, culture, and commerce cannot be understated. Thousands of years before European colonists came to these shores, Indigenous peoples had tapped maples from Newfoundland to Northern California to produce sap that was boiled to create sugar and syrup. They taught the English and French trappers how to cut V shapes into the trees and let the sap drain into birch buckets.

All maple trees produce sap; however, not all maple trees produce the same type of sap or the same level of sweetness. Lighter maple syrups have a more delicate flavor, while darker syrups have a bit more savoriness and mineral aftertaste. Grade A ratings refer to how that syrup scores on a sweetness scale. Most syrup comes from the sugar maple, but black, red, silver, bigleaf, and boxelder maples all provide nectar from their trunks when the sap runs beginning in early spring.

Beans
Mahskochiithaki

According to many historical sources, about 70 percent of the precolonial Native American diet was either foraged (wild onions, maple sap, berries) or cultivated (beans, corn, squash) from plants. For the Kickapoo, a tribe descended from the Woodland cultures of the Great Lakes region, beans have been a critical component of our foodways for nearly eight hundred years, which makes them the youngest of the Three Sisters in terms of cultivation.

The beans I most often cook with are the tepary beans grown in Arizona. They come in a variety of colors, from white and black to a marbled cranberry shade. All beans, though, are very important to the health of our bodies as well as the land. They can grow in arid environments, like that of the American Southwest. Climbing beans help cornstalks remain stable and replenish the soil with nitrogen. Corn planted alone and as a monoculture depletes soil's nutrients. Beans and corn cooked and served together contain all nine essential amino acids without any meat necessary. Beans are low in fat and sugar, and high in soluble fiber, which makes them a powerful deterrent to chronic inflammatory diseases such as diabetes and high blood pressure. They are one of nature's most versatile gifts.

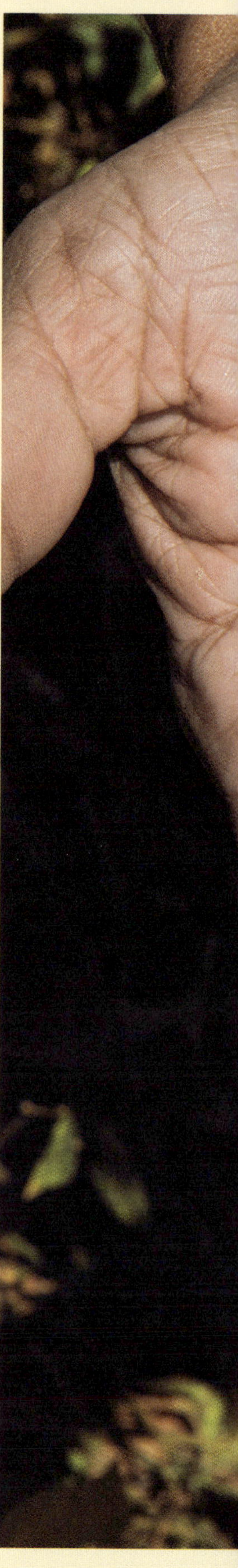

TEPARY BEAN DIP WITH PINE NUTS AND HOMEMADE CHIPS

Tepary Mahskochiithaki Pakaanani

SERVES 4 TO 6 This dip reminds me of a Mediterranean hummus made from chickpeas. It has a similar texture but is slightly more dense and has a sweeter taste from the roasted pine nuts, which have a buttery quality to them. As a midmorning or afternoon snack, the beans pack a lot of protein for energy and fullness without spiking your blood sugar. Serve the dip with tortilla chips, toasted pita bread, or raw vegetables, or plop a scoop on the Three Sisters Veggie Bowl (page 43).

1 cup white tepary beans, cooked and cooled (see page 43)

¼ cup roasted pine nuts, plus 2 tablespoons for serving

¼ cup olive oil, plus more for drizzling

Pinch of sea salt

1 recipe homemade tortilla chips (see page 88), for serving

▸ Blend the tepary beans and pine nuts in a food processor until they are broken into small pieces. While the food processor is running, slowly pour the oil into the mixture and blend until smooth. Add the salt and pulse to season the dip.

▸ Transfer the dip into a bowl, cover, and chill until ready to serve. Sprinkle the dip with the reserved pine nuts and a drizzle of oil. Serve with the crispy homemade tortilla chips.

▸ Store any leftover dip in an airtight container in the refrigerator for up to 1 week.

GIFTS FROM THE PINE TREE

Pine nuts come from two species of pinyon pine that grow throughout the American West, from Southern California and Arizona to New Mexico, Utah, Colorado, Idaho, and Wyoming. Much of this area where these scrubby "dwarf conifers" grow is called the Great Basin. The pine nuts are released from mature cones in the late summer and early fall. For thousands of years, pine nuts served as a primary food source for Native Americans, providing dense nutrients and cultural significance as well.

According to research organizations the pinyon pines, which can live up to six hundred years, are expanding their acreage beyond the one hundred million acres they occupy, creating more dense and older forested areas that are less productive.

Beyond being a food source, pines were long used by Native Americans for their medicinal properties. Porter Shimer's book *Healing Secrets of the Native Americans* documents how tribes used the resin from pine trees to make a chewing gum to soothe sore throats. The resin also was used to ease the pain of arthritic joints. Pine bark ground into a poultice healed burns and other wounds. The needles brewed into a tea helped treat chest colds and headaches.

THREE-BEAN SALAD

Neowi Mahskochiithaki

SERVES 4 I typically make a pot of beans to use in many different dishes, from the Three Sisters Veggie Bowl (page 43) to the Kickapoo Chili (page 206). This salad is a wonderful use for a mix of white, brown, and black beans. Colorful plant foods are often the healthiest, and this cool, bright, flavorful salad is full of fiber and phytonutrients that help prevent cancers and heart disease. This salad is ideal for bringing to a potluck supper, the kind we have every Wednesday at the Intertribal Friendship House. If chard is not available, substitute peppery arugula or dandelion greens, both of which are powerful digestives that help clean impurities from the body.

- ¼ cup white tepary beans
- ¼ cup brown tepary beans
- ¼ cup black tepary beans
- 1 teaspoon sea salt
- 1 pound (2 bunches) Swiss chard, chopped
- ½ medium red onion, diced
- ¼ cup pure maple syrup

▸ Rinse and sort the white, brown, and black tepary beans and soak them in water to cover for 1 hour prior to cooking. Drain the beans well, then fill a large saucepan with 8 cups water, the salt, and beans. Bring the water to a boil over high heat, then reduce the heat to low. Cover and simmer the beans for about 2 hours, until tender.

▸ Drain the beans through a colander, then let them cool completely.

▸ Layer the chard, onion, and beans in a large bowl. Drizzle with the maple syrup and toss the ingredients together. Serve the salad as a main course or as a side to salmon fillets (see page 236).

THREE-BEAN CHILI

Neowi Mahskochiithaki Chipitiini Nepoopii

SERVES 4 TO 6 This chili offers another colorful, health-filled, and simple one-pot meal that is scalable to stretch and feed a lot of people. This recipe calls for ground bison, but it can be adapted as a vegetarian version just by leaving the bison out. Something to note: I use California bay leaves that come from the bay laurel trees native to Northern California and that can be purchased or foraged. They have round leaf tips and smooth edges. Most store-bought bay leaves are from Mediterranean bay laurels, and they have pointed tips and ruffled edges. California bay leaves are more pungent and must be used sparingly, although the young leaves taste milder.

- ¼ cup white tepary beans
- ¼ cup brown tepary beans
- ¼ cup black tepary beans
- 2½ teaspoons sea salt
- 2 teaspoons olive oil
- 1 pound ground bison (optional)
- 4 bell peppers (green, red, and yellow), stemmed, seeded, and diced
- 1 large yellow onion, coarsely chopped
- 1 teaspoon freshly ground black pepper
- 3 garlic cloves, smashed and coarsely chopped
- 1 fresh California bay leaf

▸ Rinse and sort the white, brown, and black tepary beans and soak them in water to cover for 1 hour prior to cooking. Drain the beans well, then fill a large saucepan with 8 cups water, 2 teaspoons of the salt, and the beans. Bring the water to a boil over high heat, then reduce the heat to low. Cover and simmer the beans for about 1½ hours, or until just tender.

▸ Heat the oil in a medium skillet over medium heat. Add the bison (if using) and brown for 4 to 5 minutes, breaking it up into crumbled pieces. Transfer the meat to the pot of beans.

▸ In the same skillet, sauté the bell peppers and onions for about 4 minutes. Season with the remaining ½ teaspoon salt and the pepper. Add the garlic and sauté for another minute, or until the scent of the garlic blooms. Transfer the aromatics to the pot of beans and add the bay leaf. Simmer the chili for at least 30 minutes, until the beans are tender and the flavors have melded together. Ladle the chili into a bowl and savor its goodness.

GOOD MEDICINE

According to Edible Monterey Bay and other plant guides, the leaves of California bay laurel (*Umbellularia californica*) were woven by Native Americans into headbands to treat headaches or brewed into tea to lessen the discomfort of sore throats and toothaches. Poultices from ground leaves reduced inflammation from achy joints and insect bites and treated head lice. Native Americans would also use the pungent leaves in bedding to chase away biting insects like fleas and include leaves in acorn stores to keep away pests.

ANOTHER BAY LAUREL DELICACY

A jar on my yellow shelves holds a treasure trove of bay nuts gifted to me by people who come into the restaurant. The bay nut was a traditional food to the Ohlone people, who lived for thousands of years along the shores and in the hills between Monterey and San Pablo Bays. The Ohlone people, comprised of about fifty different tribes, were subjected to enslavement by Catholic missionaries, genocide during westward expansion, and the stripping of recognition by the federal government. I am always aware that I live on Ohlone land and try to honor the people by how I cook with ingredients that have fed them for centuries.

The fruit of the bay laurel is a cross between an olive and an avocado with a pit in the middle. The flesh of the fruit is edible once peeled, but the pit is a real delicacy, which can be pressed into oil, ground, or eaten. After being dried, roasted, and shelled, these shiny, dark brown nuts—about the size of hazelnuts—taste like pure unsweetened dark chocolate. They make a great snack and, when ground, an even better addition to a mole sauce.

Decolonize
WANDERING
STARS
A novel

CEDAR-SMOKED REFRIED BEANS

Pahteewi Ihskopahaakani Mahskochiithaki

SERVES 4 If you have leftover beans from any of the previous dishes in this chapter, consider mashing and recooking them with smoked cedar salt for an addition to tacos, tostadas, or as a side dish. My favorite version uses pinto beans, which have this artfully marbled outer skin before cooking, like the pinto (or painted) horses of the American West. Wildly aromatic, cedar imparts an earthy, rustic flavor indicative of this region because of the prevalence of red cedar trees throughout Northern California into the Pacific Northwest and Alaska. Cedar has strong antibacterial properties and is a powerful treatment for lung infections. Its leaves boiled for tea can help with breathing problems as well as purifying the air inside a home.

4 cups cooked pinto beans (see page 43), drained and cooled

1 tablespoon smoked cedar salt (see Resources, page 291), or more if needed

1 teaspoon olive oil

▸ Combine the pinto beans and smoked salt in a food processor and blend until the mixture is chunky-smooth. Slowly pour in the oil while the mixture processes on low speed and blend for 2 to 3 minutes, until the mixture resembles the texture of hummus.

▸ Transfer the blended beans to a medium saucepan over medium-high heat and cook for 3 to 4 minutes, adding water, 2 tablespoons at a time, as needed, to keep the beans from drying out. When the beans have reached the desired texture and temperature, taste and add more smoked salt, if necessary. Serve with Native Corn Tortillas (page 84) or alongside White Fish Tostadas (page 237).

Note

One cup of dry beans yields about 3 cups of cooked beans. To get 4 cups of pinto beans, you will need 1⅓ cups of dry beans.

LAND BACK AND THE SOGOREA TE' LAND TRUST

When I started Wahpepah's Kitchen, first as a catering business, then as a restaurant, I spoke into being three intentions:

To acknowledge that we live on stolen land.

To reclaim native foodways by promoting food sovereignty.

To educate and inform communities on the health benefits of Native American foodways.

One of the organizations that supported me from the beginning and worked alongside me in fulfilling these intentions is the Sogorea Te' Land Trust, an urban Indigenous women–led nonprofit that facilitates the return of Native American land to Native American people. My auntie Johnella is one of the co-founders of this organization, along with Corrina Gould. While they work to "rematriate" land, they also work to instill cultural knowledge, language, and practices that were lost to colonization. I will always be grateful to them for believing in my dreams.

Corrina and Auntie Johnella's fight to save sacred Native American lands was born in 2011, when they organized an encampment on the Sogorea Te', a 3,500-year-old Karkin Ohlone village and burial site in the city of Vallejo, California, which was permitted for development. For more than a hundred days, Indigenous people, many from Oakland, stood vigil and tended a sacred fire. Ultimately, they succeeded in saving much of the land through a conservation easement. But as Johnella says, the land saved them and reestablished a connection between California's Native American community and the land that was once theirs.

In 2015, Corrina and Johnella founded the land trust. Ever since, they have rematriated several pieces of land that serve to reawaken the spiritual relationship we have with the land. On a quarter-acre site in East Oakland, the Lisjan Ohlone ceremonial site, the land trust cultivates traditional and medicinal plants, such as sage and soap root, as well as fruits and vegetables. The crops are fed through a rainwater catchment system. The land trust also provides an emergency food distribution hub to those in need.

Since 2018, in West Oakland, they have grown fruits and vegetables on land saved in partnership with the Northern California Land Trust. They have saved a house and intend to restore it as an affordable and sustainable living space for elders in the community, created an urban garden in Berkeley, and secured a retreat center in the ancestral territory of the Coast Miwok and Southern Pomo people.

One of the places I love to go to restore myself is in the hills above Oakland off Skyline Boulevard where there is a piece of rematriated land now called Rinihmu Pulte'irekne (Sequoia Point). Here, you forget you are ten minutes away from the city.

It took five years of meeting every other week with the city to convey the cultural conservation easement on Sequoia Point to the land trust. The former grassland is covered with invasive species such as Monterey pine, cypress, and olive and eucalyptus trees that were planted by the poet for whom the park is named. And the old lookout point, closed off for decades, has been damaged by extreme bikers and teens who built fires. The job of the land trust now is to restore the natural habitat through traditional practices, which will help with naturally suppressing potential fire hazards, and restoring walls and walking trails. The last time I went there with Auntie Johnella, she showed me where the eagles and hawks had returned, as well as all kinds of deer. Eventually, the site will be used for teaching native practices, such as regenerating native plants, foraging for food and medicines, and the art of traditional basket weaving.

Corn
Methiikwaki

No vegetable or grain is more associated with Native American culture than corn. The plant originated within the Americas near Mexico more than seven thousand years ago. According to the National Park Service, there are 250 kinds of corn, but Native Seeds/SEARCH has recorded more than 500 different accessions of corn, representing the largest category of seeds in its bank. Popcorn and flint corn are the base for grits, hominy, coarse cornmeal, and a drink called atole, which is similar in taste to the spicy-sweet horchata made from rice milk. Flour corns are softer, come in multiple colors, and are ideal for pozole and other stews and soups. Sweet corn can be eaten right off the cob. Dent, or field, corn is heavy and large and the most prevalent among industrial growers for use in animal feed, corn syrup, and ethanol.

Because corn is a pillar of Native American sustenance, it holds great significance spiritually and medicinally in many tribal communities. Historically, in late summer before harvest, Woodland tribes celebrated the Green Corn Ceremony, which involved fasting, sweating impurities from the body, and asking forgiveness from Creator and those people you have harmed. At the end of a reverent week of gratitude and renewal, there was a feast and stomping. Women dressed in their bright ribbon skirts "swept" the dance area clean, the drumming and chants grew louder, and ecstatic dance began. This ceremony, which we had to hide until laws passed in the late 1970s allowed us once again to practice our ceremonies and religious traditions, sets us in right relation to the earth, its gifts, and to one another. There are versions of this ceremony and dance performed during powwows throughout the year.

When I was growing up in California and Oklahoma, we ate the sweet yellow corn that has come to dominate U.S. crops, but we prepared it the same way as had the ancestors. We cut the kernels from the cob, spread them out in an even layer, and dried them in the sun to "roast" them. These kernels were boiled whole in stews or ground into a porridge or used as a thickener in soups.

When I began to cater events, I met the Native American seed savers who had preserved heritage varietals of corn, beans, and squash. These Native producers graciously shared with me their red, green, and yellow Kickapoo corn from Kansas and their blue corn from the Ute Mountain range in Colorado so that I could feed my community, and my community could taste their history and begin to heal from generations of separateness.

After my mother passed, my adopted Oklahoma aunties—cousins Carol and Leslie—gifted to me the seeds of my family's Kickapoo corn, which grows into tight, sweet, tiny, deep red (almost burgundy) kernels. When someone passes their seeds to you, there are certain protocols to follow, because these are not foods grown for the masses that you can easily find in a grocery store. And the history of saving these seeds—hiding them in the hems of skirts during relocation—means they are precious and priceless. I have prayed over these seeds and asked for permission from my family and my tribe to begin growing them for the restaurant menu. Whatever recipe I create to showcase these heirlooms will honor their spirit.

BLUE CORN MUSH WITH MIXED BERRIES

Peeskipaateeki Methiikwaki Meekateethichik Miinaki

SERVES 2 Blue corn literally gets to the heart of indigenous foodways. It is versatile, vivid, and filling. Plus, it offers 20 percent more protein than yellow corn and has a lower glycemic index, which means it reduces inflammation throughout the body. Paired with fresh berries—"miinaki" in Kickapoo—steeped in pure maple syrup to bring out its essential sweetness, and topped with crisp pumpkin seeds, this breakfast (or dessert!) is a powerhouse that is good for both your heart and soul.

1 cup fresh blueberries, plus more for serving

1 cup fresh blackberries, plus more for serving

2 tablespoons pure maple syrup

1 cup blue cornmeal

¼ teaspoon sea salt

1 tablespoon toasted pumpkin seeds (see page 188), for serving

SUGGESTED TOPPINGS

A heaping tablespoon of yogurt

A teaspoon of puffed amaranth

A tablespoon of raw sunflower seeds

A drizzle of blueberry sauce

A sprinkling of dried edible flower petals

▸ Stir the blueberries and blackberries together in a medium bowl. Pour the maple syrup over the berries and stir them together. Allow the berries to macerate for at least 30 minutes or overnight in the refrigerator.

▸ Pour the macerated berries into a blender and pulse until smooth.

▸ Bring 2 cups water to a rolling boil in a small saucepan over high heat. Stir the blue cornmeal and salt into the water and cook for 3 to 5 minutes, until they form a fine porridge.

▸ To serve, divide the blue corn mush between 2 medium bowls. Divide the berry purée between each bowl, then top with fresh blueberries and blackberries and the pumpkin seeds and serve.

GOOD MEDICINE

You can add all kinds of "medicinal food" to this dish. If you are feeling down, try adding some fresh or dried rose petals for an emotional lift (as well as an immunity boost). If you need some beautiful antioxidants to protect your cells from free radicals, try adding Juneberries (*Amelanchier alnifolia*). If you want to add protein and texture to your corn mush, add some unsalted roasted mixed nuts. You can also add combinations of these "medicines" for extra healing power.

BLUE CORN FRITTERS

Peeskipaateeki Methiikwaki

MAKES 12 The best way I know how to describe these fritters is that they are like the hush puppies you find at seafood restaurants. They have that same tender crumb wrapped in a crunchy coat. These, however, are much lighter because they are made with wild rice flour, which means they are gluten-free and packed with lots of vitamins and minerals. The rice flour, along with the pecan or oat milk, gives them a bit of a nutty profile complemented by the sweet pungency of wild onions and garlic.

- 6 to 8 cups sunflower oil
- 1 cup blue cornmeal
- 1 cup wild rice flour (see Resources, page 293)
- 1 teaspoon baking powder
- ½ teaspoon baking soda
- ¼ teaspoon sea salt
- ⅓ cup wild onions (6 to 8; white and green parts), finely chopped
- ⅓ cup garlic cloves (about 12 medium), finely chopped
- 1 large egg, lightly beaten
- ½ cup pecan or oat milk

▸ Heat the oil in a large deep-sided skillet until it reaches 375°F on a candy/deep-fry thermometer.

▸ In a large bowl, whisk together the cornmeal, rice flour, baking powder, baking soda, and salt. Fold in the wild onions and garlic. Stir in the egg and pecan milk until combined. The mixture should resemble a stiff cornbread batter. Let the batter rest at room temperature for 5 minutes.

▸ Line a plate with paper towels.

▸ Scoop the batter using a 1½-inch ice-cream scoop or large serving spoon and gently place the fritter into the oil, frying it on all sides until golden brown all over, about 5 minutes total. Transfer the fritter to the prepared plate to drain. Repeat with the remaining batter. Serve with the Catfish Stew (page 232) or Bison Stew (page 199).

BLUE CORN WAFFLES

Peeskipaateeki Methiikwaki Chaakisii Pahkwesikani

SERVES 4 Ground blue corn looks a little like ash, but when it is baked into a bread or waffle, it takes on the shade of periwinkle. That purplish hue is one of my favorite colors, and it makes any dish it is in stand out. Duck eggs, which are becoming easier to source from specialty markets, add a lot of protein and lift to batter. If you cannot find duck eggs, substitute 2 large chicken eggs. Either way, these waffles turn out airy with crisp edges and are ideal to serve to friends who follow a vegetarian diet or for people with gluten sensitivities. They are also dairy-free.

- 1 large duck egg
- ¾ cup oat or pecan milk
- 1 cup blue cornmeal
- ½ cup gluten-free all-purpose flour
- 2 tablespoons pure maple sugar (see Resources, page 291)
- 1 teaspoon baking powder
- ½ teaspoon sea salt
- ¼ cup vegetable oil
- 1 recipe Blueberry Sauce (page 202) or pure maple syrup

▸ Preheat your waffle maker according to the manufacturer's instructions. (If you don't have a waffle maker, you can use this recipe for pancakes.)

▸ Whisk the egg and oat milk together in a medium bowl.

▸ In a larger bowl, stir together the cornmeal, flour, maple sugar, baking powder, and salt. Make a well in the center.

▸ Pour the egg mixture into the well, then stir the ingredients together until just combined. You don't want to overmix the batter or the waffles will come out chewy.

▸ Brush some of the oil onto the waffle maker's plates, then pour the batter into the waffle maker until it is at least three-quarters full. Close the lid and wait for the steam to stop or the indicator light to signal the waffle is ready. Remove the waffle and repeat until all the batter is gone, brushing the plates as needed. (You can keep the waffles warm and crisp, uncovered, on a baking sheet in a 200°F oven, until ready to serve.)

▸ Serve warm, drizzled with the blueberry sauce or maple syrup or both.

CORN PANCAKES WITH WILD ONIONS

Methiikwaki Chaakisii Pahkwesikani Saakahneehaki

SERVES 4 Corn and cassava starch are the foundations of flatbreads found throughout South and Central America, whether for tortillas or pancakes. Tapioca flour is made from the cassava plant, a subtropical root vegetable also known as yuca. It is naturally gluten-free, yet it is a good thickener in soups, sauces, and puddings, and a fine substitute for wheat flours and cornstarch. Indigenous cultures have long relied on easy, savory flatbreads to fill and fuel them for hours of labor. This recipe calls for wild onions, which I love for their pungency, but you can substitute scallions or spring onions.

½ cup tapioca flour

½ cup fine yellow or white cornmeal

1 teaspoon baking powder

1 teaspoon sea salt

⅓ cup finely chopped wild onions (6 to 8; white and green parts)

1 large egg, lightly beaten

3 tablespoons olive or vegetable oil

▸ Whisk together the tapioca flour, cornmeal, baking powder, and salt in a large bowl. Fold in the wild onions, then stir in the egg, which will act as an emulsifier to hold the pancakes together.

▸ Heat the oil in a large skillet or flat grill pan over medium-high heat for about 2 minutes so that it is good and hot. Scoop the batter using a 1½-inch ice-cream scoop or large serving spoon onto the pan's surface and flatten it slightly. Repeat however many times you can with at least 2 inches between each pancake so that you'll have enough room to turn them.

▸ Once the edges of the pancakes look dry, turn them over and cook until they are golden brown on both sides and fluffy. Repeat until all the batter is used. (You can keep the pancakes warm and crisp, uncovered, on a baking sheet in a 200°F oven, until ready to serve.)

▸ Serve fresh and warm as a side to the Bison Roast with Chokecherry Rub (page 209) or for brunch with thin slices of apples or pears.

CRACKED CORN WITH BLACKBERRY-MAPLE SAUCE

Methiikwaki Meekateethichik Miinaki Thiithapaakwamisi

SERVES 4 Late spring and early summer in the Bay Area is surprisingly cold, and I am an early riser. On those mornings when I have extra time, I make this comforting bowl. The corn requires soaking overnight, so it does need some planning. The texture is a cross between creamed corn and stone-ground grits and shows off the versatility of this grain. The blackberry-maple sauce is the only sweetening you will need.

1 cup cracked corn (see page 43)

1 teaspoon sea salt

FOR THE BLACKBERRY-MAPLE SAUCE

1 cup fresh blackberries (see Note), plus more for serving

2 tablespoons pure maple syrup

Note

Feel free to substitute raspberries, blueberries, huckleberries, or strawberries, depending on what berries are in season.

You can use frozen berries, but thaw and rinse to release any of the extra water that may be stored in them before using.

▸ Place the cracked corn in a bowl and cover with cold water. Allow it to soak overnight in the refrigerator. This step will soften the corn and make it easier to cook.

▸ Drain the corn and place it with 3 cups water and the salt in a large saucepan over high heat. Bring the water to a boil, reduce the heat to low, and simmer the corn, covered, for about 1 hour, until tender and the consistency of porridge. Stir the corn occasionally and add more water, if necessary. Remove the corn from the heat and let it rest while you make the sauce.

To make the blackberry-maple sauce

▸ Place the blackberries and maple syrup in a medium saucepan over medium heat. Stir the blackberries occasionally with a wooden spoon and mash them as they get softer and release more juice. Simmer for 7 to 10 minutes, until the sauce is thick and shiny. (At this point, you can leave it as is or, if you want a smoother, less textured sauce, you can strain it through a fine-mesh sieve into a bowl or measuring cup.)

▸ To serve, divide the corn evenly among 4 bowls and top with ¼ cup of the sauce. Sprinkle with a few fresh blackberries and enjoy on a cool, late-summer morning.

GOOD MEDICINE

Corn offers healing properties as well. Brewed into tea, corn silks create a soothing elixir for minor colds and digestive upset; ground, they are a salve for burns and scrapes.

SWEET BLUE CORNBREAD WITH HUCKLEBERRY COMPOTE

Peeskipaateeki Methiikwaki Piipihskiihi Miinaki

SERVES 6 TO 8 Whenever anyone asks me what huckleberries look and taste like, I always tell them a huckleberry is like a fancy blueberry. Unlike a blueberry, however, a huckleberry is small, glossy, and tart, with a flavor profile somewhere between a cranberry and a currant. The sourness of the huckleberries, served warm atop a sweet corn cake made from blue cornmeal and ancient amaranth, is tempered by the honey. You can substitute maple syrup if it is more readily available, and maple cream for the Huckleberry Compote.

FOR THE HUCKLEBERRY COMPOTE

2 cups fresh or frozen huckleberries

1 tablespoon honey

FOR THE CORNBREAD

1 cup blue cornmeal

1 cup amaranth flour (see Note)

1 tablespoon baking powder

1 teaspoon sea salt

1 large egg, lightly beaten

1 cup almond or oat milk

¼ cup pure maple syrup

Note

I make my own amaranth flour from the plants we grow at Heron Shadow. The organic company Azure Standard sells amaranth flour online at azurestandard.com and Bob's Red Mill offers an organic whole grain amaranth flour at bobsredmill.com.

To make the huckleberry compote

▸ Bring the huckleberries and honey to a boil in a medium saucepan over medium-high heat, stirring occasionally. Allow the berries to soften, break open, and thicken, about 7 minutes.

▸ Remove the compote from the heat and let it rest until ready to serve.

To make the cornbread

▸ Preheat the oven to 350°F. Butter or oil a 9-inch square baking pan.

▸ Stir together the cornmeal, amaranth flour, baking powder, and salt in a large mixing bowl. Make a well in the center.

▸ Add the egg, almond milk, and maple syrup to the well, then stir the batter together until all the ingredients are combined. (You can also use a hand mixer on medium speed.)

▸ Pour the batter into the prepared baking pan. Bake the cornbread for 35 to 45 minutes, until it has turned golden brown and the edges have pulled away from the pan.

▸ Allow the cornbread to cool in the pan on a wire rack for about 20 minutes before cutting it into squares. Place the squares on individual plates, then spoon the huckleberry compote over the cornbread for a sweet ending to a light meal.

BLACKBERRY CORNBREAD PUDDING

Meekateethichik Miinaki Methiikwaki Piipihskiihi

SERVES 6 TO 8 If you like cobblers or buckles, you will love this cornbread pudding. It bakes up with a golden, craggy terrain where the berries create trails and valleys of sweet, juicy goodness. The cakey consistency has a crisper, crunchier texture than a typical baked pudding, and its pale blue color plays off the deep purple of the berries. By using cornmeal and amaranth flour, this dessert is gluten-free, dairy-free, and vegetarian.

1 cup blue cornmeal

1 cup amaranth flour (see Resources, page 291)

1 tablespoon baking powder

1 teaspoon sea salt

2 large eggs, lightly beaten

2 cups almond, pecan, or oat milk, or buttermilk

½ cup sunflower oil

¼ cup pure maple syrup

1 pint (2 cups) fresh blackberries (see Note)

Note

Feel free to substitute other berries when they are in season. Blueberries, especially, make beautiful indigo rivers through the crust.

▸ Preheat the oven to 350°F. Butter or oil a 9-inch square baking pan.

▸ Stir together the cornmeal, amaranth flour, baking powder, and salt in a large mixing bowl. Make a well in the center.

▸ Add the eggs, almond milk, oil, and maple syrup into the well, then stir the batter together until all the ingredients are just combined. The texture will be gritty. Fold the blackberries into the batter.

▸ Pour the batter into the prepared baking pan. Bake the pudding for 35 to 45 minutes, until the top has turned golden brown and the edges have pulled away from the pan.

▸ Allow the pudding to cool in the pan on a wire rack for about 20 minutes before spooning it into 6-ounce cups to serve slightly warm but not scalding. You can drizzle it with Maple Cream (page 58) for added texture and a hint of sweetness.

GOOD MEDICINE

Until Europeans came to the Americas, native diets derived their starches from corn, amaranth, wild rice, potatoes, squash, and ground nuts and seeds, which were used to create oils, flours, and milks. Gluten proteins from wheat, barley, and rye were not part of Native American foodways until the nineteenth century, after forced displacement, which is when the prevalence of diabetes, heart disease, and cancer, as well as gastrointestinal disorders and depression, began to appear.

NATIVE CORN TORTILLAS

Methiikwaki

MAKES 12 I know it is easier to buy tortillas from the market or a tortilleria. But understanding the process that creates these versatile envelopes and getting to that masa-infused essence gives you a deep appreciation for the craft and ingenuity of the ancestors as well as elevates tacos and tostadas above "street food" status. You cannot use regular cornmeal to make tortillas or you will get a gummy paste. You must have masa harina, which involves a nixtamalization process that creates what we know as hominy from dried corn kernels. That hominy is ground—coarsely for what becomes grits or more finely for polenta or masa harina. This process breaks down the outer shell of the kernels, releasing more of their nutrients and making those nutrients more readily absorbed by the body. Masa harina is also what gives tamales their distinctive and earthy corn flavor (see Notes).

1 tablespoon slaked lime, such as pickling lime (often called "cal")

3 cups dried flint corn kernels

2 teaspoons sea salt

Masa harina, as needed

▶ Make a slurry of the slaked lime and 1 tablespoon water in a stockpot. Add the corn kernels to the pot, cover with 6 cups cold water, and stir. Set the pot over medium-high heat and bring the water to a boil. Reduce the heat to low and simmer the corn for about 45 minutes, until it grows tender but not mushy.

▶ Remove the pot from the heat, cover it, and let it rest overnight at room temperature. Add more water, if needed, to keep the corn submerged.

▶ Drain the corn through a colander and rinse under cold running water while rubbing the corn briskly between your fingers to separate the bran from the kernels.

▶ Transfer the corn to a food processor, add the salt, and grind on high until the corn has the consistency of a thick paste and there are no large pieces of corn remaining. Add as much water as needed while grinding to keep the dough from getting too dry.

▶ Scrape the dough into a mixing bowl and press it together, adding masa harina, if needed, to get the smooth consistency of clay without any dry edges. Form the dough into golf ball–size balls and slightly flatten.

▸ Set each ball between sheets of wax or parchment paper on a tortilla press (see Notes, below) and press the balls into rounds about 4 inches in diameter and no more than ¼ inch thick. To get the best results, sometimes it helps to do two presses: the first one about halfway, then turn the tortilla halfway and press fully. Practice to see what technique gives you the best results. Make sure the edges are not too thin. Stack the tortillas, separated by sheets of parchment paper.

▸ At this point, you could chill the tortillas in a plastic bag until you are ready to cook and serve. They will keep for up to 3 or 4 days, which allows you to make them ahead of when you need them.

▸ When you are ready, remove the tortillas from the fridge (if you made them in advance) and let them come to room temperature. Line a basket or bowl with a clean kitchen towel or have a tortilla warmer at the ready.

▸ Preheat a skillet over medium-high heat and place a tortilla in the skillet. Cook for 30 seconds, or until the edges of the tortilla lightly brown. Flip the tortilla and cook the other side. Transfer the tortilla to the basket or warmer and cover. Repeat until all the tortillas are done.

▸ Serve immediately with Smoked Squash Tostadas with Green Chili Salsa (page 121) or Sweet Potato and Smoked Hibiscus Taquitos with Tomatillo Salsa and Hibiscus Sauce (page 181).

Notes

If you want to skip grinding the corn, you can substitute 2 packed cups masa harina in this recipe.

If you don't have a tortilla press, place the tortilla dough balls between 2 pieces of wax or parchment paper and press flat using a heavy cast-iron skillet.

VARIATION

TOSTADAS AND TORTILLA CHIPS

- Line a baking sheet with paper towels.
- Heat 4 cups vegetable oil in a Dutch oven to between 350° and 375°F on a candy/deep-fry thermometer over medium-high heat.
- For tostadas, leave the uncooked tortillas whole. For chips, cut the uncooked tortillas into quarters. Gently place the tortilla/quarters into the hot oil and fry until crisp and golden brown, 3 to 5 minutes. Remove the tortilla/chips from the oil with a slotted spoon and drain on the prepared baking sheet. Sprinkle generously with coarse sea salt and allow them to cool.
- Enjoy them alone or with any of your favorite dips, such as the Tepary Bean Dip with Pine Nuts (page 62) or the Smoked Salmon Dip with Red Chilies (page 241).

DRIED HOMINY WITH WILD TURKEY SOUP

Takwahaani Peneewa Nepoopii

SERVES 4 TO 6 This soup mirrors a pozole, a stew with a hominy base in traditional Mexican cuisine with roots in the pre-Columbian era. A pozole is studded with chicken or pork and garnished with crisp, cool vegetables such as cabbage or avocados. It is essential to soak the sun-roasted corn overnight in cold water. Bee balm (*Monarda fistulosa*) is an indigenous member of the mint family with a flavor similar to that of oregano. In fact, if you cannot find dried bee balm through a specialty grocer, you may substitute the same amount of dried oregano in this recipe.

- 2 cups heirloom hominy or pozole, covered with cold water and soaked overnight in the refrigerator
- 2 tablespoons olive oil
- 2 pounds wild turkey breast (see Note), cubed
- 1 teaspoon sea salt
- 1 teaspoon freshly ground black pepper
- ½ medium yellow onion, chopped
- 4 garlic cloves, coarsely chopped
- 2 teaspoons ground bee balm or dried oregano
- 2 fresh California bay leaves

▸ Drain the hominy through a colander and set aside.

▸ Line a plate with paper towels.

▸ Heat the oil in a large stockpot over medium heat. Sprinkle the turkey breast cubes on all sides with the salt and pepper, then brown the meat on all sides in the oil for 7 to 10 minutes. Transfer the meat with a slotted spoon to the prepared plate.

▸ Sauté the onion in the oil and tasty bits left in the pot over medium heat for about 5 minutes, until tender. Add the garlic and sauté for 30 seconds to allow the scent to blossom. Add the hominy, meat, bee balm, bay leaves, and 12 cups cold water to the stockpot and bring to a boil. Reduce the heat to low, cover, and simmer the soup, stirring occasionally, for 3 hours, or until the hominy is tender.

▸ Ladle the soup into bowls and serve. Store any leftovers in an airtight container in the refrigerator for up to 1 week.

GOOD MEDICINE

Bee balm, or wild bergamot, is an amazing antimicrobial medicine native to the Americas. Not only is it beloved by pollinators and hummingbirds, but it is also edible and effective in treating all kinds of bacterial infections, from strep throat to pneumonia. The flower petals can be dried and brewed for tea to soothe an upset stomach or menstrual cramps. The dried leaves can be ground and mixed with elderberry, honey, and vinegar for a cough suppressant. Leaves can be made into a poultice or mixed with oil to create a salve for burns, scrapes, and cuts.

FRIED HOMINY IN DUCK FAT

Takwahaani Siisiipe'a

SERVES 4 My grandmother made fried hominy for breakfast almost every morning, serving it with potatoes and eggs. I prefer white cracked corn hominy that has been made from an heirloom flint, a harder corn than dent, as its name suggests, with less soft starch in its kernels. Because of its density, hominy lends itself to roasting and grinding for the production of grits and polenta. Hominy is foundational to indigenous diets throughout South, Central, and North America.

- ¼ cup duck or bacon fat
- 1 cup pearl hominy, cooked according to package instructions
- ⅛ green or red bell pepper, stemmed, seeded, and finely chopped
- ⅓ medium white onion, finely chopped
- 1 teaspoon sea salt
- ½ teaspoon freshly ground black pepper

▸ Melt the duck fat in a large sauté pan over medium heat. Add the hominy, bell pepper, and onion and cook for 7 to 10 minutes, stirring frequently, until the vegetables are tender and slightly browned.

▸ Serve as part of a hearty breakfast or as a warm, comforting side to the Bison Roast with Chokecherry Rub (page 209).

GOOD MEDICINE

Bell peppers are a mild member of the *Capsicum* genus. Although they are low in capsaicin, bell peppers are super high in important nutrients such as vitamin C, vitamin A, and fiber. They are wonderful for relieving congestion and inflammation in the lungs. They are also useful in lowering blood pressure, bad cholesterol, and blood sugar.

HOMINY SALSA AND TORTILLA CHIPS

Takwahaani and Methiikwaki

SERVES 4 Salsa is one of the easiest and healthiest snacks to make. This one still packs that fresh-from-the-garden tomatoey goodness, while incorporating the intense flavor of hominy. I like mine chunky, but you can chop the ingredients finer for a smoother consistency. Aside from serving it with chips, hominy salsa makes the ideal accompaniment to scrambled eggs or as a condiment for tacos or tostadas.

- 6 Roma tomatoes, seeded and diced
- ½ large red onion, diced
- ½ cup cooked hominy (see page 43)
- 2 garlic cloves, finely chopped
- Juice of 1 lime
- 3 tablespoons chopped fresh cilantro
- ½ teaspoon fresh oregano leaves
- ⅛ teaspoon sea salt
- ⅛ teaspoon ground cumin
- Homemade tortilla chips (see page 88) or pita, for serving

TIP

Toss in ½ cup of cooked white tepary beans (see page 43) for added texture, flavor, and a big protein punch.

▸ Vigorously toss the tomatoes, red onion, hominy, garlic, lime juice, cilantro, oregano, salt, and cumin in a medium bowl so that the tomatoes can release all their juices and talk with the lime and seasonings. Cover the bowl and let it rest in the fridge for at least 30 minutes.

▸ Serve with the tortilla chips for a cool, crunchy appetizer. Store leftovers in an airtight container in the refrigerator for up to 1 week.

Notes

Specialty meat markets and your favorite hunters are the best places to source wild turkey breast. Feel free to substitute farm-raised turkey, beef, bison, or venison for the wild turkey called for in this recipe or to mix and match. This thick, hearty soup pairs well with roasted squash blossoms (see page 119), leftover roasted squash (see page 43), and other seasonal root vegetables.

ROASTED HEIRLOOM CORN SOUP

Methiikwaki Nepoopii

SERVES 4 This recipe is a homage to my Sac and Fox grandmother. It was one of the first dishes I learned to make in the kitchen with her and my aunts. We always started to make this soup by cutting the kernels from white field corn and letting them dry on screens in a single layer in the sun for three or four days. This soup is ubiquitous in one form or another throughout Native Country during harvest season. It is a celebration food seen at powwows and community centers in Oklahoma. It is the cornerstone of our menu at the restaurant because Wahpepah's Kitchen would not be the same without this filling, flavorful, smoky soup, which I make with heirloom Kickapoo corn from Kansas Kickapoo. There are two ways to achieve subtle smokiness with the corn: roast it in the oven with wood chips or use a smoking gun (see Note) to infuse it. Both approaches are explained here.

6 ears fresh green corn, kernels cut from the cob

3 pounds chuck roast, cubed

2 teaspoons sea salt

1 teaspoon freshly ground black pepper

1 small yellow onion, cut into medium dice

1 cup cubed pumpkin squash

4 to 6 cups Vegetable Stock (page 97), or water

TIP

You can substitute 2 cups dried heirloom corn for the fresh green corn in the recipe. Just soak the kernels overnight and drain them well before roasting them according to the instructions.

To roast the corn

▶ Preheat the oven to 425°F. Line a baking sheet with aluminum foil.

▶ Spread the corn kernels in a single layer on the prepared baking sheet. Place 3 tablespoons wood chips on the same baking sheet and light them to char and get them to smoke.

▶ Place the baking sheet in the oven and roast the corn for 20 to 25 minutes, until lightly browned and tender. Set aside until ready to add to the soup.

To make the soup

▶ Heat the oil in a Dutch oven or stockpot over medium-high heat. Season the meat with salt and pepper.

▶ Add the corn, the meat, the onion, and the squash, and cover with the vegetable stock or water. Bring the soup to a boil, then reduce the heat to low and simmer, covered, for 2 hours.

▶ Ladle the soup into 4 to 6 large bowls and serve with Frybread (page 99).

▶ Store any leftovers in an airtight container in the refrigerator for up to 4 days.

Continued

Note

Culinary smoking guns are available for as low as $40 and as high as $150. We use them in the restaurant to add layers of flavor to vegetables and fruits. The smoking gun will not give you the same depth as, say, a whole chicken or bison brisket slow-roasted all day over a fire in a smoker, but it will infuse a hint of pecan, oak, mesquite, or any other wood of choice without a lot of fuss.

Smoking guns look a little like kitchen torches with a long hose attached. You simply fill the chamber with wood chips, light the chips, turn on the fan, and smoke billows from the hose. To smoke the corn, we place the kernels in a sealable bag, fill it with the smoke, and seal it for a few minutes to allow the corn to absorb the flavor.

VEGETABLE STOCK

MAKES 12 CUPS (3 QUARTS)

- 1 celery stalk, cut into 2-inch chunks
- 1 pound carrots, cut into 2-inch rounds
- 1 large white onion, quartered
- 1 whole garlic head, peeled and smashed
- 1 fresh California bay leaf
- 1 tablespoon sea salt

▸ Place the celery, carrots, onions, garlic, bay leaf, and salt in an 8-quart stockpot and cover with 12 cups water. Bring to a boil over medium-high heat. Reduce the heat and simmer the vegetables, covered, for 1 hour. Remove the stockpot from the heat and let the stock cool to room temperature.

▸ Remove the vegetables from the water and strain the broth into pint- or quart-size containers. Store what you don't need right away in the freezer for up to 6 months so that you have some on hand anytime you want to make a soup or stew, or a savory corn dish, or for rice.

FRYBREAD

Keetahteehi

SERVES 4 TO 6 I debated whether to include a recipe for frybread in this book because it is a food that fills many Native Americans with conflicting emotions. It was a survival food made necessary only because of the forced displacement of Native peoples and the commodities food program by the U.S. government. I do not include frybread on the menu in the restaurant and serve it only sparingly when I make this soup or upon request by a catering client. In the end, though, I felt I would not pay proper respect to my grandmother or the memory of making soup with her without honoring our making frybread by hand together. That memory is comforting to me, as frybread was in times of scarcity. Its remaking as sustenance shows the ingenuity of our people.

- 3 cups all-purpose flour, plus more for forming the dough
- 3 tablespoons baking powder
- 1 tablespoon sea salt
- 2 cups sunflower oil

▸ Combine the flour, baking powder, and salt in a large mixing bowl. Fluff the flour with your hands, then add 1½ cups warm water a little bit at a time, mixing it into the flour until the mixture comes together into a sticky dough. Let the dough rest for 30 minutes.

▸ Heat the oil in a deep-sided skillet to 375°F on a candy/deep-fry thermometer. Line a plate with paper towels.

▸ With your hands powdered with flour, form the dough into 2-inch balls. Pat each ball into a flat disk and make a hole in the center. Gently lay it into the hot oil and cook on each side for 2 to 3 minutes, until golden brown. Remove the frybread from the oil using tongs and set the breads on the prepared plate to drain.

▸ Serve as a side to favorite soups or stews. The frybread should have a crunchy exterior with a soft, chewy interior, much like a sopapilla or beignet.

Wahpepah's Kitchen

GREEN CORN CAKES

Aaskipakiyaaki Methiikwaki Chaakisii Pahkwesikani

SERVES 4 TO 6 Green corn does not refer to the color of the kernels but to the stage of the corn's growth at the time it is picked. Green corn should be among the first ears harvested, with tight, lettuce-colored husks; moist, flaxen silks; and tiny kernels closely packed together. The corn's texture is creamier, which gives these pan-seared cakes an almost hoecake quality. These cakes make a hearty starter served with a slather of Huckleberry Compote (page 81) or a tasty side to wild turkey or venison.

- 4 ears fresh green corn
- Pinch of sea salt
- ½ cup gluten-free all-purpose flour
- 2 tablespoons vegetable or olive oil

▸ Shuck the corn and cut the kernels away from the cob. Place the corn kernels in a food processor and pulse until they make a smooth paste. Add the salt and flour to the corn and pulse until well blended.

▸ Heat the oil in a large skillet or griddle pan over medium-high heat. Ladle or use a 1½-inch ice-cream scoop to place the corn batter into the pan. It will look like a thick pancake. Once the edges start to dry and lift, after about 2 minutes, flip and cook the other side until golden brown. Repeat the process with the remaining batter.

▸ Serve one or two cakes per person.

GOOD MEDICINE

Did you know that huckleberries have antiviral properties? If you collect the glossy green leaves of the huckleberry bush in the spring and summer, use a tea infuser to steep the leaves in hot water for 5 minutes or longer, depending on the desired strength, then mix in a tablespoon of local raw honey. The tea helps clear the lungs of congestion from allergies and colds. Huckleberry juice has been used to ameliorate sore throats.

Because huckleberries pack a high amount of fiber in their tiny packages, they regulate digestive health, which can also aid with regulating blood sugar.

BLUE CORN CUPCAKES

Peeskipaateeki Methiikwaki Chasskisii Pahkwesikani

MAKES 12 Want to bring a dessert that will enchant everyone at your next potluck picnic or party? These cupcakes disguise their more nutritional qualities while they maintain a tender crumb because of the puréed squash, which acts as an emulsifier instead of using oil or butter. The berries are like a hidden treasure inside. Instead of piles of overly sweet frosting, the maple cream drizzle and edible flower decoration make pretty packages of these deceitfully healthy desserts.

- 1½ cups amaranth flour (see Resources, page 291)
- 1½ cups blue cornmeal
- 1 teaspoon baking powder
- 1 teaspoon sea salt
- 1 cup coconut milk
- 1 large duck egg
- ¼ cup puréed squash (see Tip, page 118)
- 2 tablespoons pure maple sugar (see Resources, page 291)
- 2½ cups fresh, frozen, or cooked berries, such as blueberries or blackberries
- Maple Cream (page 58), for serving
- Edible flowers, for garnish

▸ Preheat the oven to 350°F. Line a 12-cup muffin tin with parchment liners or coat each cup with coconut oil.

▸ Whisk together the amaranth flour, cornmeal, baking powder, and salt in a large bowl. Make a well in the center.

▸ In another bowl, mix together the coconut milk, egg, squash purée, and maple sugar.

▸ Pour the coconut milk mixture into the well. Mix the cupcake batter with a large wooden spoon or hand mixer until everything comes together.

▸ Arrange berries in the bottom of each muffin cup, then pour equal amounts of batter into each of the cups, covering the fruit completely and filling to about three-quarters full.

▸ Bake for 40 minutes, or until a toothpick inserted into the center of the cupcakes comes out clean. Allow the cupcakes to cool in the pan for 15 minutes before removing them from the pan.

▸ You can serve them lightly warm or let them cool completely. Drizzle with the maple cream and serve with an arrangement of edible flowers on top.

INDIGENOUS DUMPLINGS WITH BERRIES

Piipihskihii Miinaki

SERVES 4 TO 6 Berries are as indigenous to American landscapes as are my people. That is why you'll find them in savory as well as sweet dishes, powdered for medicinal purposes, and crushed for dye. They are a staple of our diets—and they are my jam. This simple recipe is evocative of a traditional stovetop cobbler with pillowy biscuit-like dumplings. The natural sweetness of the blueberries and blackberries is heightened by all-natural unsweetened grape juice and pure maple syrup. Served warm from the stovetop, this dish is both comforting and invigorating—and a window into my story with food.

- 1 cup fresh blueberries, plus more for serving
- 1 cup fresh blackberries, plus more for serving
- 1 cup unsweetened grape juice
- ¼ cup pure maple syrup
- 1 cup white cornmeal
- ¼ cup all-purpose flour
- 1 teaspoon sea salt
- 1 teaspoon baking powder
- 1 large duck egg, lightly beaten

▸ Bring the blueberries, blackberries, grape juice, and maple syrup to a boil in a large saucepan over medium heat. Reduce the heat to low and simmer for 5 to 7 minutes, until the fruit begins to break apart and the juices thicken.

▸ Whisk together the cornmeal, flour, salt, and baking powder, then stir in ½ cup room-temperature water and the egg to create a sticky dough.

▸ Spoon the dough into the simmering berries and cook the dumplings for 10 to 15 minutes, until they are cooked through and fluffy.

▸ Serve the fruit dumplings warm or at room temperature, with a few fresh berries.

BLUE CORN THUMBPRINT COOKIES

Peeskipaateeki Methiikwaki Kohkisaani

MAKES 24 These cookies are a hit at catering events because they are not only eye-catching—and we eat with our eyes first—but also they are sweet without being cloying or overfilling. Fair warning: I do use butter because a squash purée would hold too much water in the dough and would not allow enough air to give the dough a lift. The butter gives the dough a richness too. These cookies have much more texture than flour-based cookies, and they can stand up to a cup of tea. The preserves give them a sweet-tart balance. If you want to save time, feel free to use a store-bought preserve or jam. Red Lake Nation makes wonderful wild blueberry jam, chokecherry jelly, and wild hawthorn jelly. Learn more in the Resources (page 291) at the end of the book.

FOR THE JAM FILLING

1 cup fresh blackberries, blueberries, or raspberries

2 tablespoons pure maple sugar (see Resources, page 291) or raw local honey

1 teaspoon freshly squeezed lemon juice

FOR THE COOKIES

1½ cups finely ground blue corn flour

1 cup amaranth flour (see Resources, page 291)

2 teaspoons cornstarch

½ cup pure maple sugar (see Resources, page 291)

1 teaspoon sea salt

1 cup (2 sticks) unsalted butter, at room temperature

1 large duck egg

1 teaspoon pure vanilla extract

To make the jam

▸ Bring the blackberries, maple sugar, and lemon juice to a boil in a medium saucepan over medium-high heat. Use the back of a fork or a potato masher to smush the berries and release their juices. Once the berries have come to a boil, reduce the heat to low and continue to simmer for 10 to 15 minutes, until the berries have a more jellylike consistency. Remove the pan from the heat and let the jam cool while you make the cookie dough.

To make the cookies

▸ Preheat the oven to 350°F. Line 2 baking sheets with parchment paper.

▸ Whisk together the corn flour, amaranth flour, cornstarch, maple sugar, and salt in a large bowl.

▸ Cream the butter in the bowl of a stand mixer fitted with the paddle attachment or with a hand mixer on medium-high speed for about 3 minutes, or until the butter is light and fluffy. Reduce the speed to medium and beat in the egg and vanilla until just incorporated. Reduce the speed to low and beat in the flour mixture until the dough comes together.

▸ I like to use a small (1½-inch) ice-cream scoop to make the balls uniform in size so that they bake evenly. Scoop the dough into balls and set the cookies 2 inches apart on each baking sheet. Press your thumb into the center of each ball to create an indentation to fill with the berry jam.

▸ Bake the cookies on the middle rack of the oven for 8 to 10 minutes, until the edges are slightly brown. Allow the cookies to cool on the pans on wire racks for 5 minutes before transferring them to wire racks to finish cooling completely.

INDIGENOUS POPCORN BALLS WITH EDIBLE FLOWERS

Methiiwaki Peeskoneiihi

MAKES 12 So much of who I am today started in Fruitvale. I went to elementary school at Lazear, where my fifth-grade teacher, Ms. Rinehart, let me bring whatever I made at home to school on Fridays. More often than not, I made popcorn balls—we called them Crystal Balls then—and I sold them for fifty cents each. So, this recipe has been in my arsenal for a long time. When Apple Studios asked me to cater its premiere for *Killers of the Flower Moon,* I knew popcorn balls with bright yellow sunflower petals would weave a bit of my story with the story of the Osage murders that took place in Oklahoma during the 1920s. Sunflowers grow abundantly across the Oklahoma landscape and play a large part in the state's agricultural industry. Native Americans have been using the seeds, petals, and oils of sunflowers in cookery for thousands of years. While these Crystal Balls cannot tell you the future, I can tell you they make great treats for Indigenous Peoples' Day, the second Monday of October.

2 teaspoons sunflower oil

1¼ cups pure maple syrup

1 teaspoon sea salt

1 cup indigenous popcorn

1½ cups dried edible flowers, such as sunflower petals

Note

I purchase all-natural, non-GMO popcorn kernels from the Lower Brule Sioux Tribe on the Missouri River. You can too at lakotafoods.com.

▸ Spray or brush a baking sheet with 1 teaspoon of the sunflower oil.

▸ Heat the maple syrup and salt in a medium saucepan over low heat, stirring occasionally, until a candy/deep-fry thermometer reads 230°F.

▸ Slowly pour the syrup over the popped corn in a large bowl and toss until all the kernels are evenly coated, then toss with the edible flowers until evenly distributed.

▸ Coat your hands with the remaining 1 teaspoon sunflower oil and form the popcorn into tight balls about the size of tennis balls. Place the balls 1 to 2 inches apart on the prepared baking sheet to dry completely.

GOOD MEDICINE

Sunflowers not only boost your mood just by looking at them or by arranging them in a vase for your table, but the sum of their parts is also greater than their bright, beaming wholes because every part of the flower is edible.

Sunflower seeds are the fruit of the flower, with a single seed inside the husk. That tiny seed holds an abundance of vitamins and minerals and healthy fats. We have to get our B vitamins—thiamine, riboflavin, niacin, folate, biotin, cobalamin, and others—from food because our body does not naturally produce them. These essential vitamins, however, support energy levels, memory, and mood, and prevent blood deficiencies such as anemia. The vitamins A and E in the seeds support vision and nerve health. Selenium helps not only with digestion but also boosts metabolism. The seeds, when added to cereal or salads or as a snack, help regulate blood sugar, hormone balances, and immune function.

The petals and leaves are full of vitamin A and, when freshly picked, enliven salads and stews, or when dried, are steeped for tea.

REGENERATING INDIGENOUS AGRICULTURE WITH THE CULTURAL CONSERVANCY

When I returned to Oakland after living in Oklahoma for fourteen years, I became close friends with Melissa K. Nelson (Turtle Mountain Chippewa), then the first Native American executive director for The Cultural Conservancy (TCC). TCC, which was founded in 1985 and became Native-led in 1992, has promoted Native rights globally and helped record oral histories and songs to create a library of resources that tell our stories, among so many other important programs it sponsors. The work that TCC has done to preserve and foster Native American foodways has been central to my own mission to reclaim our foods and our health.

Through land purchases, perpetual conservation easements, and partnerships, TCC has saved lands to regenerate indigenous agriculture. As a member of the Indigenous Seed Keepers Network, TCC participates in native seed exchanges that get heirloom seeds back into the hands of tribal members through its Native Seed Library. The seed keepers gather these seeds from all corners of Turtle Island—from elders' homes, from other Native American farmers and organic seed savers, from research institutions, and from the government, the latter having "held captive" native seeds for generations—and protect them from efforts by industrial agricultural conglomerates to claim intellectual property over the seeds or to prevent Native communities from growing their own foods. These seeds are our inheritance and our children, the key to food sovereignty. Yet, they always are in danger of being taken again. According to the Organic Seed Alliance, 60 percent of the world's seed stock is controlled by only four companies.

In 2022, TCC acquired nearly eight acres of land in Sonoma County that is part of the territories of the Coast Miwok and Southern Pomo peoples of the Federated Indians of Graton Rancheria. At Heron Shadow farm they grow chilies, tomatoes, Hopi black beans, blue-speckled tepary beans, Quapaw red corn and Pawnee corn, as well as the Buffalo Creek squash, miner's lettuce, and amaranth that I use in the restaurant. Most of the produce is distributed to eight community sites, such as the Intertribal Friendship House, the Native American Health Center, the Sonoma County Indian Health Project, and the California Indian Museum & Cultural Center, before the remainder is sold at farmers' markets. Those who tend the farm do so with great care, ensuring that every action honors the water and nourishes the soil so that the food grown there nourishes us and fights what are called lifestyle diseases—as if diabetes, depression, high cholesterol, and high blood pressure were choices and not a result of the bad agricultural practices that have stripped food, water, and soil of their nutrients.

Through my relationship with TCC, I have traveled to Hawai'i for its annual Food & Wine Festival to participate in an indigenous food panel. In September 2024, I traveled to Turin, Italy, with members of the Native American delegation sponsored by Tamalpais Trust for the Terra Madre Salone del Gusto, an international exchange organized by Slow Food. This trip helped connect my story with that of other Indigenous communities around the world so that we can work together to preserve and protect what is authentically ours to cherish.

Squash
Aapikooni

For thousands of years, Indigenous peoples have cultivated squash in the Americas. Archaeological evidence shows squash farming in Mexico as far back as 7,500 years ago. There are more than one hundred types of gourds, squash, and pumpkins worldwide, with twenty plus varieties native to South, Central, and North America. Tribes in the Northeast grew pattypan squash. Acorn squash was prevalent among the Great Plains tribes. Hubbard squash first appeared near the Andes Mountains before making its way north. Chayote grew during the 1100s near Guatemala. Even the squash blossoms were delicacies. With their brightly colored skin and thick yellow and orange flesh, squash just radiate abundance and hope. The way squash supports the health of other plants through its own growth demonstrates a symbiotic relationship with the land and Creation.

One of the greatest gifts I have received are seeds for Buffalo Creek squash from the Seneca Nation of western New York. They were given to me by Sara Moncada, formerly with The Cultural Conservancy. Boldy orange and ginormous, Buffalo Creek squash, a type of Hubbard squash with a small, crooked neck, is one of the original Three Sisters. On land owned by The Cultural Conservancy, Heron Shadow farm in Sonoma, I invited my staff to help plant these seeds so that we could grow and harvest them for the restaurant. Every member of the front- and back-of-house team showed up early on a Saturday morning to get their hands in the dirt. We saved the seeds from the first crop, and those have since gone into the ground. We have repeated that cycle for three seasons now. One day soon we will add corn and beans to this plot of land where the Ohlone once lived—another step toward transforming our legacy, by recalling who we were before colonization and rebuilding our strength through traditional foods.

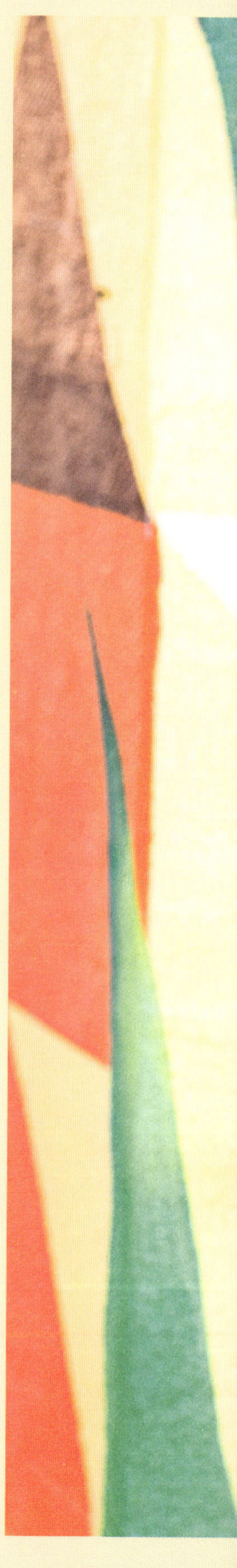

ACORN SQUASH WITH MAPLE AND PECANS

Mehtekomini Aapikooni Pakaana

SERVES 4 TO 6 Acorn squash get their name from their shape. They have a dull, dark green skin with some patches of yellow or orange and are most readily available from early fall through the winter months. Choose those that are heavy and firm with no soft spots. Store them in a cool, dark place, like a cupboard, until ready to use. They lend themselves to both sweet and savory dishes because of their mild, nutty flavor.

1 medium acorn squash

½ cup sunflower oil

¼ cup pure maple syrup, for drizzling

½ cup coarsely chopped pecans, for garnish

▸ Preheat the oven to 400°F. Line a baking sheet with parchment paper or brush it with sunflower oil.

▸ Wash the squash with warm soapy water, then rinse it well and dry completely with a towel. Use a large sharp knife to trim both ends of the squash. (It takes a bit because the skin is tough and the flesh is dense.) Stand the squash on one of the flat ends and cut the squash in half lengthwise. Scoop out the pulp and seeds with a large spoon and set aside to toast the seeds later for a snack (see Tips).

▸ Lay the flat side of the halved squash down on a cutting board and slice it into ½-inch half-moons. Repeat this step with the other half. Lay the slices on the prepared baking sheet and drizzle with the oil. Toss the slices so that all surfaces of the squash are coated.

▸ Roast the squash for 30 to 45 minutes, until golden brown and tender.

▸ Arrange the slices on a platter. Drizzle with the maple syrup, sprinkle with the pecans, and serve warm as a side to Cheyenne River Steak (page 213).

VARIATION

ROASTED ACORN SQUASH SOUP

SERVES 4 TO 6

1 cup roasted pecans

1 whole acorn squash

1 tablespoon pure maple syrup

½ teaspoon sea salt

▶ Soak the roasted pecans in 1 cup cold water for at least 1 hour, until they soften. Transfer the pecans to a food processor or blender and purée. Strain the purée through a fine-mesh sieve into a bowl.

▶ Preheat the oven to 400°F. Line a baking sheet with parchment paper or brush it with sunflower oil.

▶ Wash the squash with warm soapy water, then rinse it well and dry completely with a towel. Use a large sharp knife to trim both ends of the squash. (It takes a bit because the skin is tough and the flesh is dense.) Stand the squash on one of the flat ends and cut the squash in half lengthwise. Scoop out the pulp and seeds with a large spoon and set aside to toast the seeds later for a snack (see Tips).

▶ Lay the squash, cut-sides down, on the prepared baking sheet. Roast the squash for 30 to 45 minutes, until golden brown and tender. Allow it to cool until it is comfortable to handle.

▶ Scoop the squash from the skins into a blender or food processor. Add the maple syrup, salt, and pecan purée, then purée it all until silky smooth.

▶ Divide the soup among 4 to 6 bowls and serve warm with a slice of Roasted Squash Blossom Cornbread (page 119).

TIPS

The seeds of any squash or pumpkin make a great snack, so do not throw them out. Remove the seeds from the pulp. Wash them and let them dry on paper towels. Toss them with 1 tablespoon sunflower oil and 1 teaspoon sea salt, and spread them in a single layer on a parchment-lined baking sheet. Preheat the oven to 275°F and toast them for 15 to 20 minutes, until golden brown.

For a sweeter version, toss the seeds with 1 tablespoon pure maple syrup and 1 tablespoon sunflower oil before toasting them.

The seeds are supercharged with magnesium, which supports more than three hundred different cellular reactions in the body. The vitamin A, beta carotene, and potassium help with blood pressure, heart arrythmia, and eyesight. The fiber aids digestive issues.

Notes

Feel free to substitute pecan milk, if you can find it in the supermarket, for the pecan purée.

Butternut, kabocha, and delicata squash can all substitute for either recipe if acorn squash is not available.

SMOKED SQUASH PURÉE

Pahteewi Aapikooni

SERVES 4 Squash purée can be made throughout the year, using whatever squash is in season. Full-bodied squash—butternut, Hubbard, and Buffalo Creek—lend themselves well to the purée, as do sugar pumpkins. This sweet-savory-salty side serves as an ideal accompaniment to Bison Roast with Chokecherry Rub (page 209) or on a tostada (see page 88). To achieve the desired intensity of smokiness, you can either roast the squash with wood chips as here or use a smoking gun (see page 96).

1 (5-pound) Buffalo Creek squash, halved and seeded

2 tablespoons olive oil

1 tablespoon pure maple syrup

1 teaspoon sea salt

½ teaspoon freshly ground black pepper

TIP

If you do not want that smoky flavor, simply forgo using the wood chips or a smoking gun and proceed with the recipe.

- Preheat the oven to 325°F. Line a baking sheet with parchment paper.
- Brush the cut sides of the squash with the oil, then lay the squash halves, cut-sides up, on the prepared baking sheet.
- Place 1 cup mesquite wood chips on a baking sheet and light them to get them to char and smoke. Set the dish with the chips on the lower oven rack. Place the baking sheet on the upper rack. Bake the squash for 30 to 45 minutes, until tender. Allow it to cool until it is comfortable to handle.
- Scrape the squash into a food processor with 2 tablespoons water, the maple syrup, salt, and pepper. Pulse to purée, adding more water (up to ¼ cup total) to achieve the desired consistency.
- Serve chunkier on Smoked Squash Tostadas with Green Chili Salsa (page 121) or velvety and smooth as a soup.
- Store cooled leftovers in an airtight container in the refrigerator for up to 3 days.

GOOD MEDICINE

People do not often think of squash as being a medicinal food. However, various members of the species *Cucurbita maxima* have been shown to function as a safe anti-parasitic as well as an excellent blood tonic. Additionally, winter squash serves as a diuretic, helping the body to expel excess fluids.

ROASTED SQUASH BLOSSOM CORNBREAD

Aapikooni Methiikwaki Piipihskihii

SERVES 6 TO 8 The sunset-golden flowers of squash, especially spaghetti and zucchini squash, are delicious, like a brighter, grassier version of the squash they come from. They can be stuffed and fried, which is a staple of Italian cookery, or sautéed in a little bit of sunflower oil and sprinkled with salt and pepper, or tossed into a salad. I love them roasted, just on their own, or baked into a cornbread. I get most of my edible flowers from Sakari Farms, an Inupiaq-owned and -operated farm in Bend, Oregon, that grows traditional foods from ancestral seeds (see Resources, page 291).

½ cup squash blossoms

1½ cups amaranth flour (see Resources, page 291)

1½ cups yellow or white cornmeal

1 teaspoon baking powder

1 teaspoon sea salt

1 large duck egg

¼ cup olive oil

▸ Preheat the oven to 115°F. Line a baking sheet with parchment paper.

▸ Rinse and dry the squash blossoms. Lay them in a single layer on the prepared baking sheet. Roast for 6 hours, or until the blossoms are dried and crumbly. (You can also use a food dehydrator machine for this step.)

▸ Allow the blossoms to cool before crumbling or flaking them for the cornbread batter.

▸ When you are ready to prepare the cornbread, preheat the oven to 375°F. Wipe a cast-iron skillet with sunflower oil.

▸ Whisk together the amaranth flour, cornmeal, baking powder, and salt in a large bowl. Make a well in the center.

▸ Add the egg and olive oil into the well, then stir the batter together until just combined.

▸ Pour the batter into the prepared skillet and sprinkle the roasted squash blossoms over the top of the batter. Bake the cornbread for 20 to 30 minutes, until golden brown. Once the cornbread is cool enough to handle but still slightly warm, cut it into squares and serve with the Kickapoo Chili (page 206) or Dried Hominy with Wild Turkey Soup (page 90).

SMOKED SQUASH TOSTADAS WITH GREEN CHILI SALSA

Pahteewi Aapikooni Aaskipakiyaaki Chipitiini

MAKES ½ CUP, SERVES 4 TO 6 At this point in the book, you are starting to see how different recipes form the building blocks of a variety of dishes with new flavors added in. Stretching ingredients is a Native American specialty. Smoked squash is one of those foundational dishes in indigenous cooking, and here it is paired with a bright, savory salsa made with roasted tomatillos. Tomatillos are those green tomato-looking fruits covered in papery brown husks in the produce aisle. They may be new to you, but the Aztecs, according to several sources, were cultivating these in Mexico nearly three thousand years ago.

FOR THE GREEN CHILI SALSA

1 tomatillo, roasted (see Tip) and chopped

1 jalapeño pepper, stemmed, seeded, and diced

1 garlic clove, coarsely chopped

¼ cup chopped fresh cilantro

1 teaspoon ground cumin

½ teaspoon pure maple sugar (see Resources, page 291)

½ teaspoon sea salt

1 recipe Smoked Squash Purée (page 118), for serving

1 recipe homemade tostadas (see page 88), for serving

▸ Combine the tomatillo, jalapeño, garlic, cilantro, cumin, maple sugar, and salt in a blender or food processor and purée until smooth.

▸ To serve, spread a generous tablespoon or more of warm smoked squash purée on each warm tostada, then drizzle with the cool salsa. The taste sensation is smoky-sweet with just a bit of spicy heat.

TIP

How to roast tomatillos: Preheat the oven to broil. Remove the husks of 6 tomatillos, then wash and dry the tomatillos. Slice them in half horizontally and place them, cut-sides down, on an oiled baking sheet. Brush the tomatillos with vegetable oil. Broil for 10 to 12 minutes, until the green skins have begun to blister and char.

You can also roast tomatillos over a heated grill or gas stove flame, turning them until the skin has blistered and charred.

Chop the tomatillos once they are cool enough to handle.

SQUASH CAKES

Aapikooni Chaakisii Pahkwesikani

MAKES 12 These crisp patties are a great way to get healthy vegetables into your pickiest eaters. The crackle on the outside belies the soft (squashy) interior. The green, orange, and deep purple color palette reminds me of sunset across a Northern California landscape in early autumn. The wild rice flavor imparts a bit of earthy nuttiness, and the cranberries punctuate the cakes with sparks of natural sweetness.

4 zucchini, stemmed and shredded

6 scallions (white parts), thinly sliced, green parts reserved for garnish

½ cup roasted squash, finely diced (see page 43)

1 cup wild rice flour (see Resources, page 293) or gluten-free all-purpose flour

¼ cup olive oil

¼ cup dried cranberries

1 tablespoon sea salt

▸ Preheat the oven to 350°F. Line a baking sheet with parchment paper.

▸ Combine the zucchini and sliced scallions in a large bowl and mash together. Transfer to a fine-mesh sieve set over another bowl and press to release all the moisture, so that the mixture is as dry as possible.

▸ Return the mixture to the large bowl and stir in the squash, wild rice flour, oil, cranberries, and salt until the ingredients are well blended. Let the mixture rest for 10 to 15 minutes.

▸ Use a large (3 tablespoons) ice-cream scoop to create individual cakes and place on the prepared baking sheet. Flatten the cakes with the palm of your hand. Bake the squash cakes for 12 to 15 minutes, until golden brown.

▸ Garnish the squash cakes with the reserved scallion tops. Serve immediately as a starter or as a side to Maple-Roasted Turkey Wings (page 224).

SQUASH PUDDING

Aapikooni

SERVES 4 TO 6 Almost any fruit can be transformed into a plush, glossy, and decadent pudding, but squash lends a warm, comforting touch—especially because here it is twice baked. Although dairy-free, this pudding offers the expected level of creaminess with a bit of added richness and texture from the puréed pecans. Because of its sweet-savory balance, this pudding can be served as a side dish to venison or as a dessert with a drizzle of Maple Cream (page 58).

- 1 whole butternut squash, peeled
- 1 cup pure maple syrup
- 1 cup puréed pecans (see page 117)
- ¼ cup pecan halves
- 2 teaspoons coconut oil
- 1 teaspoon pure vanilla extract

▸ Preheat the oven to 375°F. Line a baking sheet with parchment paper.

▸ Use a large sharp knife to cut the top and bottom of the squash off flat. Stand the squash on the flat end and cut it in half lengthwise. Scoop out the pulp and seeds with a large spoon and set aside to toast the seeds later for a snack (see Tips, page 117).

▸ Lay the squash halves, cut-sides down, on the prepared baking sheet. Roast the squash for 30 to 45 minutes, until golden brown and tender. Allow it to cool until it is comfortable to handle.

▸ Reduce the oven temperature to 350°F.

▸ Cut the squash into cubes, then put the cubes into a blender or food processor. Add the maple syrup, puréed pecans, pecan halves, coconut oil, and vanilla and purée the mixture until silky smooth.

▸ Pour the squash mixture into a casserole dish. Bake the pudding, uncovered, for 30 to 45 minutes, until golden brown. Serve warm.

HUBBARD SQUASH FALL SALAD WITH AGAVE VINAIGRETTE

Aapikooni Otaatopakooni Thiithapaakwamisi

SERVES 4 TO 6 All salads aren't built on a cold bed of lettuce, nor are they made to be enjoyed only on hot summer days. In fact, a warm salad of squash, lightly caramelized and sweetened by olive oil and agave syrup, makes a healthy, satisfying meal (or side) during cold winter months. The amaranth gives it a light crunch. Agave syrup derives from the same succulent that tequila does. It flourishes in the sun-drenched soils of Mexico and the Caribbean and often is mistaken for aloe. Like aloe, the thick, spiky leaves can be cut and rubbed directly on wounds for healing. Agave, however, is also a digestive that improves gut health.

1 small (10- to 12-pound) Hubbard squash, halved, seeded, and coarsely chopped

1 teaspoon olive oil

1 teaspoon agave syrup

1 recipe Agave Vinaigrette (recipe follows)

1 tablespoon puffed amaranth

▸ Preheat the oven to 325°F.

▸ Toss the squash with the oil and agave syrup in a large bowl. Spread the squash in an even layer on a baking sheet. Roast the squash for 30 minutes, or until lightly browned and tender.

▸ While the squash cooks, pour the agave vinaigrette into a large bowl. Sprinkle with the amaranth for a light crunch.

▸ Once the roasted squash has slightly cooled, toss it in the vinaigrette and amaranth. Serve warm alongside the Blueberry Bison Meatballs with Blueberry Sauce (page 201).

AGAVE VINAIGRETTE

MAKES ½ CUP

¼ cup cider vinegar

¼ cup olive oil

3 tablespoons agave syrup

1 teaspoon sea salt

▸ Whisk the vinegar, oil, agave syrup, and salt together in a small bowl.

▸ Serve tossed with salad ingredients or use as a dip for vegetables or as a marinade for meats. Store any remaining vinaigrette in an airtight container in the refrigerator for up to 2 weeks.

PUMPKIN SOUP WITH MAPLE-CHILI OIL

Kaskinwiihi Nepoopii Thiithapaakwamisi-Chipitiini Pemi

SERVES 4 For millennia, Indigenous peoples throughout the Americas depended on pumpkins as an essential part of their diets. The seeds, dried and occasionally roasted, could be carried easily for snacks. The flesh could be baked, boiled, roasted, and dried, and mashed, served in stews, or ground into flour. The edible pumpkin blossoms could be stuffed with beans, meat, or grains and roasted, or added to soups. During the period of the Columbian Exchange (1492 to 1800) and the onset of the transatlantic slave trade, pumpkins and other indigenous foods traveled across the world and encountered new culinary traditions in Africa and Europe.

This richly colored and flavored soup makes the most of autumnal fruits and vegetables. For all its robust goodness, it is easy to make and can be frozen for future use. In a cup or a bowl, it makes a warm complement to the Hubbard Squash Fall Salad with Agave Vinaigrette (page 124) and a side of Sweet Blue Cornbread (page 81).

1 (5- to 7-pound) sugar pumpkin, halved and seeded

1 large carrot, cut into 1-inch rounds

1 tart Granny Smith apple, halved and cored

1 garlic clove

1 cup coconut milk

1 tablespoon ground sumac

1 teaspoon sea salt

½ teaspoon freshly ground black pepper

Maple-Chili Oil (see Tip, page 46), for serving

▶ Preheat the oven to 325°F. Line a roasting pan with aluminum foil.

▶ Fill the prepared roasting pan with ¼ inch water. Place the pumpkin halves face down in the pan and surround them with the carrots, apple, and garlic. Roast the pumpkin for 30 to 45 minutes, until tender. Allow it to cool until it is comfortable to handle.

▶ Scrape the pumpkin meat, along with the other roasted vegetables, into a food processor and purée until smooth. Strain through a fine-mesh sieve into a Dutch oven and place over medium-low heat. Stir in the coconut milk and bring to a boil. Stir in the sumac, salt, and pepper, and cook for 15 to 20 minutes more.

▶ Serve in large bowls, with a drizzle of maple-chili oil.

GOOD MEDICINE

Garlic (*Allium sativum*) is another common culinary ingredient with important medicinal properties. Garlic is antifungal, antiseptic, and antibacterial. Adding garlic to your food on a regular basis will help lower blood pressure, improve liver function, and strengthen lungs.

The red fruits of the staghorn sumac have been used by Indigenous peoples all over the world as a spice in both savory and sweet dishes. It should not be confused with poison sumac, which has white berries on smooth branches and grows in swampy areas. Staghorn sumac is widely employed as a medicinal herb that is useful for increasing milk flow in nursing mothers and as an astringent tea, which is excellent for reducing swelling and inflammation.

PUMPKIN BREAD

Kaskinwiihi Chaakisii Pahkwesikani

MAKES 1 LOAF What whispers "fall has arrived" more than a warm slice of spiced pumpkin bread? This recipe requires a little more effort than opening a can of pumpkin purée. Instead, you will roast your own pumpkin, but the results are well worth the time for a lighter, more intense, and fruitier-flavored bread. This quick bread recipe is easily doubled so that you can keep one loaf for snacking and wrap another one to give away.

1 (1-pound) sugar pumpkin

2 cups gluten-free all-purpose flour

1 teaspoon baking soda

½ teaspoon baking powder

1 teaspoon ground cloves

1 teaspoon ground cinnamon

1 teaspoon ground nutmeg

½ teaspoon sea salt

1½ cups (3 sticks) unsalted butter, at room temperature

2 cups pure maple sugar (see Resources, page 291)

2 large duck eggs

▸ Preheat the oven to 350°F. Line a baking sheet with parchment paper or brush it with sunflower oil.

▸ Wash the pumpkin with warm soapy water, then rinse well and dry it completely with a towel. Use a large sharp knife to cut off the top of the pumpkin. (It takes a bit because the skin is tough and the flesh is dense.) Scoop out the pulp and seeds with a large spoon and set aside to toast the seeds later for a snack (see Tips, page 117). Cut the pumpkin into quarters.

▸ Lay the pumpkin quarters, cut-sides down, on the prepared baking sheet. Roast the pumpkin for 30 to 45 minutes, until golden brown and tender. Allow it to cool until it is comfortable to handle.

▸ Scoop the pumpkin flesh from the skin into a blender or food processor and purée until silky smooth. Set aside.

▸ Butter and flour one 8½ x 4½ x 2½-inch loaf pan or spray with nonstick cooking spray.

▸ Whisk together the flour, baking soda, baking powder, cloves, cinnamon, nutmeg, and salt in a large bowl.

▸ Cream the butter and maple sugar in the bowl of a stand mixer fitted with the paddle attachment on medium-high speed until light and fluffy. Add the eggs, one at a time, beating until each one is fully incorporated. Reduce the speed to low and mix in the flour mixture until almost incorporated. Raise the mixer speed to medium and beat in the pumpkin purée for 2 minutes.

▸ Pour the batter into the prepared loaf pan. Bake the bread for 45 minutes, or until it springs back to the touch and the sides have pulled away from the pan. Cool the loaf in the pan for at least 20 minutes before turning it out onto a wire rack to cool completely—or almost cool, because one of the great pleasures of pumpkin bread is that first slice from a warm loaf.

▸ If you do not devour the entire loaf, wrap the remainder in plastic wrap and keep it at room temperature for up to 4 days or in the refrigerator for up to 1 week. If you want to make multiple loaves while pumpkins are in season, you can wrap the loaves in plastic wrap then aluminum foil and store them in freezer bags in the freezer for up to 2 months.

INDIGENOUS WISDOM MEETS CLINICAL INTEGRITY AT THE NATIVE AMERICAN HEALTH CENTER

One of the reasons for writing this book is that I wanted to show how I was healed by connecting with the ceremony and celebration within this wonderful intertribal community that nurtured me as I grew up. Because of this community, the intergenerational trauma in my family ends with me and I have become an advocate for the native food essential to our well-being. What we have endured as a people is not the end of the story. Our genetic makeup is so much more than our history. I came to understand this truth the more I wandered into the fields to touch the dark soil, to listen to the blackberries, to taste the wild onions, to see the squash seeds sprout green leaves, to smell the cedar and redwood. When I returned to feed my family and my neighbors, I found my own peace of mind. Food is a spiritual endeavor.

Our ancestors understood that community, ceremony, food, and sacred spaces paved the way to wholeness, resilience, and adaptability. And for more than fifty years, the Native American Health Center (NAHC) has put these principles into practice in the heart of Oakland's inner city. Founded as the Urban Indian Health Board out of the American Indian Movement in 1972, the NAHC opened access to medical, dental, and behavioral health services that were often denied Native Americans in the Bay Area. Now, they serve multicultural and marginalized populations, using the best of Western medicine with the best of traditional wisdom.

Martin Waukazoo, a Lakota, served as the NAHC's chief executive officer for forty years. When he recognized that the center of the urban Indigenous community had blossomed in Oakland, Marty purchased the former American Indian Human Services building on International Drive and expanded the NAHC's services. He understood that leaning into the cultural touchstones of Native American people would help us beyond the pure practice of Western medicine. By buying the building, he reclaimed land for our benefit and changed the mindset from renting to owning. The current Seven Directions healthcare center is a lasting symbol of empowerment, in keeping with the idea that every decision made impacts the next seven generations. Marty gave me my first big catering job while I was still in culinary school. He changed the trajectory of my life and that of my daughters as well.

No one in the community is turned away when seeking medical treatment at the NAHC, which has grown to encompass health centers at eight of Oakland's public schools. The center's social services include youth programming, workforce development, food distribution, and rental assistance.

In 2018, the NAHC initiated the Indigenous Red Market to share the culture, build community, and establish economic pathways for Native American entrepreneurs. On market weekends, more than forty Native artisans, craftspeople, and food producers (including Wahpepah's Kitchen) fill the streets around the NAHC's facilities. Indigenous performers from around the country—comedians, musicians, dancers—entertain while also educating the more than twelve hundred visitors who gather there.

In 2024, the NAHC opened a sweat lodge in a former parking lot adjacent to the clinic. Having a sweat lodge where Native peoples can meet for ceremony and to ritually eliminate impurities is rare in an urban area and will be essential for helping our community's youth learn traditional ways.

Now under the leadership of Natalie Aguilera, an enrolled member of the Choctaw tribe, the NAHC is expanding once again to meet the needs of the greater Fruitvale area. The new building's first floor will more than double the number of dental stations currently available and provide more meeting spaces, including a three-hundred-person-capacity cultural community center. In partnership with an affordable housing developer, seventy-six apartment units will fill the upper four floors.

I serve on the building committee and am thrilled with how Native American symbols and art will inform the architecture and interiors, including public murals by Native artists, Ohlone basket-weave patterns, and the flicker headdresses of California Native dancers, all reflected in designs throughout the facility. The new fourteen-thousand-square-foot building is expected to open in late 2025.

Natalie has carried on Marty's convictions to develop leadership and decision making using the principles of ancient indigenous wisdom. Prayer, song, and celebration are integrated throughout the center's direct services and in the creation of new facilities. The street that runs between the current facility and the new building was renamed for Marty so that, as Natalie says, "his name will always be spoken."

2

FORAGED FOODS

Anesithaakeki Ithenieni

For hundreds of years, bands of Kickapoo gravitated toward the tall grass prairies near forested areas for their settlements so that they had easy access to deer and rabbit and could forage acorns, sap, berries, nuts, and seeds. After the Kickapoo were pushed first from the Northeast by the Iroquois, then from their lands in what is now Wisconsin and eastern Michigan by the Sioux, they built settlements in what is now Illinois. Continued displacement by waves of colonists and broken treaties forced bands of Kickapoo into Kansas, Oklahoma, Texas, and Mexico, where tribal members still live the traditions handed down and held on to.

One of those traditions is looking at all of nature's beings and things as having a soul and the belief that Mother Earth offers everything we need to feed ourselves, our families, and our communities. We, not just Native Americans but all of us, have been disconnected from the land for so long that we have to relearn how to live with the trees, the grasses, the fruits, and the animals in a reciprocal relationship. I grew up with family who taught me how to forage. We shuffled through underbrush for morels or wandered through brambles for ripe berries and hiked with friends through prairies and parks to learn more about which plants provide medicine just by eating their leaves or boiling their roots into teas. Foraging feeds my soul.

BERRIES
Miinaki

GREENS, TUBERS, AND SEEDS

Otaatopakooni, Ohpeniyeeki, Miinekaanani

Berries
Miinaki

Miinaki—"berries"—to me are the most beautiful food, and as strange as it may sound, I enjoy a kinship with them. They are a cornerstone ingredient in my cooking. They are responsible for my healing.

When I was five or six years old, my grandfather took me to the untamed brambles on Wahpepah land around McLoud, Oklahoma, to pick wild blackberries fattened by the warm sun. The land felt like my protector, my connection. I heard it calling to me, and I would talk with the berries and they would nourish me.

When my sister and I lived with our aunt Carleta on the Hoopa Valley Reservation in far Northern California, I found peace in picking huckleberries, blueberries, elderberries, pine nuts—whatever was in season. We would make pies, and I took comfort in that, and I took comfort in that cycle of foraging from the land and tasting its sweetness. During our time in Canada, we plucked wild strawberries from low bushes, filling our bellies with the earth's goodness.

On the outside, people may have thought we were poor, but we feasted on this seasonal bounty, and out of so many painful experiences of displacement, of being uprooted, something inside me knew that I was made to create from Creator's gifts. I cherish them, and they remain my protectors to this day. I believe life is a circle, and if berries can heal me, they can heal somebody else. And so, I have cooked with berries all my life.

BLACKBERRY SALAD

Meekateethichik Miinaki Otaatopakooni

SERVES 4 It may seem strange to have a recipe for a simple salad in a cookbook, but stay with me here. A salad made with freshly picked, organically and ethically grown (or foraged) produce, still slightly warm from the sun, is the first step—truly—to learning how our food is meant to be enjoyed and eaten, how it is supposed to really taste. Our taste buds have been conditioned by industrial-corporate systems based on profit to crave salt and sugar, but this salad has only the slightest touch of either in the dressing. Imagine, instead, eating these seasonal delights without the flavor-deadening and harmful residue of pesticides, herbicides, and fungicides. The beauty of this recipe is that you can put your own spin on it and use the seasonal greens that grow near you or in your garden and celebrate berries or other fruits as they make their annual appearance.

4 cups late-summer or early-fall greens, such as arugula, spinach, or mustard or dandelion greens

1 recipe Sage Dressing (recipe follows)

1 cup fresh blackberries

¼ cup toasted pumpkin seeds (see Tips, page 117)

2 tablespoons puffed amaranth

▸ Toss a mess of seasonal greens in a large bowl with the sage dressing. Top with the blackberries, pumpkin seeds, and amaranth. Serve on plates or individual bowls.

A WORD OR TWO ABOUT SAGE

White sage (*Salvia apiana*) is the only sage indigenous to North America. It grows throughout the Baja Peninsula and Southern California up to the area around Los Angeles. Much of its habitat has been destroyed by development, and its existing range is threatened by over picking by poachers to fuel the New Age spiritual industry, which has adopted and commodified the Native American ceremonial rite of burning white sage for purification. White sage is not used in cookery.

Mediterranean sage (*Salvia officinalis*), a member of the mint family that we grow in our gardens and use in all kinds of cooking traditions, came to North America during the early 1600s with colonists from Europe. Through trade with colonists, Native Americans began growing sage, using its leaves and roots for tea to treat everything from headaches and joint aches to sore throats, dental issues, menstrual cramps, and upper respiratory issues.

SAGE DRESSING

MAKES 1 CUP

3 fresh sage leaves

⅓ cup olive oil

¼ cup cider vinegar

¼ cup agave syrup

Pinch of sea salt

▸ Cook the sage and oil in a small saucepan over medium-low heat for 5 to 7 minutes, until the sage leaves have grown tender. This step infuses the oil with the sage's pungent, woodsy essence while also softening its intensity.

▸ Remove the oil from the heat and let it cool slightly. Blend the mixture in a blender or with an immersion blender, then strain it through a fine-mesh sieve into a bowl. Whisk the oil with the vinegar, agave syrup, and salt until combined. This dressing can be served warm or cool.

▸ Store any unused dressing in an airtight container in the refrigerator for up to 2 weeks.

VARIATION

BLACKBERRY-SAGE DRESSING

MAKES 2 CUPS

1 cup fresh blackberries

3 fresh sage leaves

⅓ cup olive oil

¼ cup cider vinegar

¼ cup pure maple syrup

Pinch of sea salt

▸ Cook the blackberries and sage in a medium saucepan over medium heat for 5 to 7 minutes, until the blackberries begin to break down and the sage leaves have softened.

▸ Remove the blackberries from the heat and let them cool slightly.

▸ Blend the mixture, then strain it through a fine-mesh sieve into a bowl. Whisk in the oil, vinegar, maple syrup, and salt until combined. Serve the dressing either warm or cold.

▸ Store any unused dressing in an airtight container in the refrigerator for up to 2 weeks.

TIP

These dressings can be used as a marinade for game birds, such as quail or pheasant, and chicken, and they can be used as a sauce over roasted root vegetables (see page 187).

SMOKED SALMON AND BERRY SALAD WITH BERRY VINAIGRETTE

Pahteewi Chaakisii Memeethaki Miinaki

SERVES 4 TO 6 This salad is ideal for summer because it is light and filling with lots of textures from creamy to crisp and flavors from tangy and bitter to charred all playing together. The smoked salmon in this recipe, however, is not like the kind you get at a supermarket or deli that has been slowly cold-smoked according to Scottish or Norwegian traditions. This salmon is thick, oily, and intensely flavored by the wood used in a shorter, hot-smoking process developed thousands of years ago by Native American tribes in the Pacific Northwest and Northern California. You can purchase the smoked salmon from some of the same sources I do, which are found in the Resources on page 291, or you can smoke your own salmon low and slow in a smoker or more quickly with a smoking gun (see the Note at the end of this recipe). Cheerful nasturtium leaves and flowers give this already colorful salad extra zing with a peppery profile.

- 1 pound mixed summer greens, such as miner's lettuce, arugula, and spinach
- 1 pound hot-smoked salmon (see the headnote and the Tip), flaked
- 2 cups fresh mixed berries, such as blackberries, blueberries, strawberries, and raspberries
- ½ cup Berry Vinaigrette (recipe follows)
- 2 tablespoons puffed amaranth
- Edible flowers, such as nasturtiums

▸ Toss the summer greens, salmon, and berries with the berry vinaigrette in a large bowl until everything is evenly coated. Sprinkle the salad with the amaranth and edible flowers.

▸ Serve family style or evenly divided among 4 to 6 plates.

TIP

For a lighter summer salad, skip the salmon and you still have a vivid array of fresh fruits and greens to enjoy.

BERRY VINAIGRETTE

MAKES 1½ TO 2 CUPS

- ¼ cup fresh blackberries
- ¼ cup fresh blueberries
- ¼ cup fresh strawberries
- ¼ cup fresh raspberries
- 3 tablespoons agave syrup
- ¼ cup cider vinegar
- ¼ cup olive oil
- 1 teaspoon sea salt

▸ Cook the blackberries, blueberries, strawberries, raspberries, and agave syrup in a medium saucepan over medium heat for 7 to 10 minutes, until the berries begin to break down. As the berries cook, press them with the back of a large spoon to help them release their juices.

▸ Transfer the berries to a blender. Add the vinegar, oil, and salt and purée until smooth. Strain the mixture through a fine-mesh sieve into a jar or bowl. Serve with the smoked salmon and berry salad or another one of your favorite salads.

▸ Store any unused vinaigrette in an airtight container in the refrigerator for up to 2 weeks.

Note

My dear good friend Morning Star Gali, a member of the Ajumawi band of the Pit River Tribe of Northern California, drops by the restaurant on occasion to bring me smoked Chinook or coho salmon from her tribe. I treasure and hoard her offerings because they are so precious and tied to our Native American heritage. She too is a treasure, as a warrior for indigenous sovereignty, historic preservation, and sacred lands protection.

When I cook salmon, I first marinate the boneless fillets in pure maple syrup and a little sea salt and freshly ground black pepper. I then bake or grill it. Then, if I want to get that burnished smokiness, I use a smoking gun (see page 96). Place cooked salmon in a sealable bag and close it about 75 percent. Fill the chamber of the smoking gun with wood chips like cherry or pecan, light them, turn on the fan, and let the smoke billow from the hose into the bag. Once the bag is filled with smoke, seal it for a few minutes to allow the salmon to absorb the flavor.

STRAWBERRY-SUMAC SALAD WITH MAPLE-SAGE VINAIGRETTE

Oteehiminani-Maakomisi Thiithapaakwamisi-Otaatopakwi

SERVES 4 Another cool, summer-season salad includes strawberries uplifted by the intrinsic citrus hints of ground sumac. This salad tastes best with either homegrown or wild strawberries (*Fragaria chiloensis, Fragaria virginiana,* and *Fragaria vesca*), which are small, juicy, and intensely sweet. Their natural abundance of ellagic acid creates a powerful barrier to insulin resistance and helps lower bad cholesterol.

6 cups spring mix lettuce

3 cups sliced wild strawberries

1 tablespoon fresh sumac

½ cup Maple-Sage Vinaigrette (recipe follows)

2 tablespoons raw sunflower seeds

2 tablespoons popped amaranth

▶ Place the spring mix and strawberries in a large bowl. Pour the vinaigrette over the greens, then toss the salad using your fingers or tongs until the vinaigrette is evenly distributed.

▶ Divide the salad evenly among 4 chilled plates, top each with the sunflower seeds and amaranth for a crispy finish, and serve immediately.

GOOD MEDICINE

A concentrated reduction made from boiling sumac berries and bark creates an antifungal extract to treat yeast infections and thrush.

MAPLE-SAGE VINAIGRETTE

MAKES ¾ CUP

¼ cup cider vinegar

¼ cup pure maple syrup

¼ cup olive oil

5 to 10 fresh sage leaves

1 teaspoon sea salt

▶ Whisk together the vinegar, maple syrup, and oil in a medium bowl. Plunge the sage into the mixture and let it rest for at least 30 minutes to infuse the vinaigrette with all the sage's herby goodness.

▶ Remove the sage, then stir in the salt until it dissolves. Use the vinaigrette as a finish on your favorite late-summer or fall salad.

▶ Store any unused vinaigrette in an airtight container in the refrigerator for up to 2 weeks.

GOOD MEDICINE

When steamed, ground wild strawberry leaves have an astringent quality that helps cleanse clogged facial pores. A tea brewed from the ground strawberry leaves can thwart colds as well as alleviate upset stomach. Likewise the medicinal benefits of blueberries aren't just contained in the deliciousness of the fruit. Tea made by steeping fresh or dried leaves from blueberry (*Vaccinium ovalifolium, Vaccinium alaskaense*) bushes helps stabilize blood sugars, settle upset stomachs, treat colic, and reduce inflammation in the eyes, even aiding with some cataracts and other vision issues.

Pineapple Sage (Salvia elegans)
Pineapple sage leaves
to make herbal tea.
and are a colorful

BLUEBERRY STEW WITH WILD TURKEY

Miinaki Peneewa Nepoopii

SERVES 4 TO 6 If you feel tired and unfocused, this rich, smoky stew will reenergize you with its dense nutrients, vivid color, and flavor. Along with being a delicious food native to North America, blueberries are incredibly nutrient-dense with high levels of vitamins C and K, and lots of fiber. Blueberries have a well-deserved reputation as a superfood because of their flavonoids, in particular, which protect your cells from oxidative stress. In addition to being enjoyed in desserts and breakfast foods, incorporating berries into savory dishes is another way of receiving their benefits.

¼ cup olive oil

1 pound smoked or roasted turkey breast, cubed

2 carrots, cut into medium dice

3 celery stalks, cut into medium dice

1 small white onion, diced

3 garlic cloves, coarsely chopped

1 tablespoon smoked cedar salt (see Resources, page 291)

1 cup fresh blueberries

1 fresh California bay leaf

6 small red potatoes, halved

1 cup cubed butternut squash

▸ Heat the oil in a large stockpot over medium heat. Add the turkey, carrots, celery, and onions and sauté for 5 to 7 minutes, until the vegetables are tender. Add the garlic and cook for 1 minute more. Season with the smoked salt, stir in the blueberries, and cook for 3 to 5 minutes more.

▸ Pour 5 cups water into the stockpot, scraping the bottom to release all the tasty bits, then add the bay leaf, potatoes, and squash. Bring the stew to a boil, reduce the heat to low, cover, and cook for 20 minutes, or until the potatoes and squash are fork-tender. Serve hot.

▸ Store any leftovers in an airtight container in the refrigerator for up to 3 days.

Notes

If you want to amp up the turkey-ness of this stew, roast 3 turkey legs in a preheated 350° F oven. Rub the turkey legs with olive oil, season with salt and pepper, and place them skin-side down on a parchment-lined baking sheet. Bake the legs for 30 minutes, turn them over and roast them for 30 to 40 minutes more, until the internal temperature reaches 165° F. (You can also substitute smoked turkey legs.)

Add the roasted turkey legs where turkey is called for in the recipe. At the point in the recipe where the stew has cooked for 20 minutes, remove the turkey legs, debone the meat, and return the meat to the stew and cook until the potatoes and squash are fork-tender.

CHOKECHERRY PUDDING WITH PUMPKIN SEED MIX

Katoowakimina Kaskinwiihi Miinekaanani

SERVES 4 Although this pudding makes a delightful finish to a meal, it makes for a healthy and satisfying breakfast too. It is gluten-free and vegan, and between the chokecherries, chia seeds, and pumpkin seed mix, you will get a wholesome dose of your daily nutrient intake—all under the guise of a tangy and creamy dessert with a bit of crunch from the topping. (See page 192.)

FOR THE CHOKEBERRY PUDDING

½ cup fresh chokecherries

¼ cup pure maple syrup

1 tablespoon cornstarch

½ cup coconut milk

¼ cup chia seeds

FOR THE PUMPKIN SEED MIX

½ cup toasted pumpkin seeds (see page 117)

½ cup popped amaranth

¼ cup toasted sunflower seeds (see Note below)

¼ cup dried sunflower petals

To make the chokeberry pudding

▸ Bring the chokecherries and ½ cup water to a simmer in a medium saucepan over medium heat. After 7 to 10 minutes, the chokecherries will begin to break down and the pits will be released to the bottom of the pan.

▸ Strain the chokecherries through a fine-mesh sieve into a bowl, then pour the strained fruit back into the saucepan.

▸ Bring the chokecherries to a boil over medium heat, stirring frequently, then add the maple syrup and cornstarch. Cook for 5 to 7 minutes more, until the pudding has thickened.

▸ Turn off the heat and stir in the coconut milk and chia seeds. Set the saucepan on a wire rack or trivet to cool and thicken the pudding further.

To make the pumpkin seed mix

▸ Toss the pumpkin seeds, amaranth, sunflower seeds, and sunflower petals together in a medium bowl.

▸ To serve the pudding, spoon it into 4 small bowls or dessert cups and top each serving with some pumpkin seed mix.

▸ Store any leftover pumpkin seed mix in an airtight container at room temperature for up to 2 weeks.

TIP

Be creative and put your personal spin on the pumpkin seed mix. Add walnut or pecan halves, crushed chokecherry patties, dehydrated blueberries, or gooseberries.

Note

To toast shelled sunflower seeds, heat a skillet over medium heat. Spread a half cup of sunflower seeds in a single layer in the skillet and toast them for 5 to 10 minutes, stirring frequently to prevent burning. Once they have turned lightly golden, remove them from the heat and let them cool completely. Store any unused seeds in an airtight container in the refrigerator.

GOOSEBERRY JAM

Miinaki

MAKES 2 CUPS Before the 1900s, grapelike gooseberries grew throughout the northeastern and north-central part of the country and up into Canada. But they were banned by the federal government after the beginning of the twentieth century because they carried a fungus that was lethal to white pine trees and, thus, to the timber industry. Even though that ban has been lifted across most of the country, Delaware, New Jersey, North Carolina, and Maine still have prohibitions against gooseberry cultivation, and they are not that easy to find.

Native Americans foraged during summer months for the globes with their translucent glassy skins that beheld sparkling juice inside. The yellow and green ones tasted sour, while the red, purple, and black ones grew sweeter as they grew darker in color. Folks enjoyed the gooseberries fresh, dried like raisins, or boiled into jams like this one.

1 pound fresh or frozen gooseberries or cranberries

1¼ cups pure maple sugar (see Resources, page 291)

TIP

You can find frozen gooseberries at supermarkets such as Trader Joes and order them from online sources such as Northwest Wild Foods.

▶ Bring the gooseberries and ½ cup cold water to a steady simmer in a medium saucepan over medium heat. Once the gooseberries grow soft, after 5 to 7 minutes, stir in the maple sugar until it completely dissolves, the water has reduced by half, and the fruit has thickened.

▶ Remove from the heat and let the jam cool to room temperature. Ladle the jam into a sterilized medium glass jar with a tight-fitting lid. Store in the refrigerator for up to 3 months.

▶ You can serve the jam warm or cold. It makes a striking and tasty condiment for an Indigenous Food Board (see page 242).

GOOD MEDICINE

American gooseberries (*Ribes hirtellum*) are in the currant family (*Ribes sanguineum*) and share many of the same health benefits. They are high in fiber and aid in weight management, and because of their calcium content they support bone health. Their vibrant colors signal strong antioxidant properties as well as immune boosters.

NATIVE BLACKBERRY PUDDING

Meekateethichik Miinaki

SERVES 4 TO 6 When it comes to pudding, most people think of a sweet, creamy confection or a puffed savory pastry. In native cultures, puddings are lightly sweet, slightly soupy, and textured with fruits, cornmeal, and seeds. Because traditional Native American diets do not include dairy or wheat, blue cornmeal is used as a thickening agent. The sweet-tart flavor is as intense as its deep purple color. It tastes like summer in a bowl.

- 6 cups fresh blackberries, plus more for serving
- ¼ cup pure maple syrup or pure maple sugar (see Resources, page 291)
- 1 tablespoon blue cornmeal
- 1 tablespoon raw sunflower seeds, for sprinkling

▸ Bring the blackberries, 1 cup water, and the maple syrup to a simmer in a large saucepan over medium-low heat. While stirring occasionally, reduce the heat to low and continue to simmer for 7 to 10 minutes more, until the berries have softened and begun to break apart. Stir the cornmeal into the berries and cook for another 5 minutes, or until the pudding thickens.

▸ Spoon the pudding into medium bowls and serve warm or chilled. Add a few fresh blackberries and sprinkle with sunflower seeds for a contrasting crunch.

Notes

Any species of blackberry can be used in this recipe, or you can substitute raspberries, blueberries, or mulberries.

Depending on where you live, honey or agave syrup may be more readily available. You can substitute either for the maple syrup called for in this recipe.

GOOD MEDICINE

Blackberries are used to treat all kinds of viral illnesses, such as colds and flu. They are excellent for promoting healthy digestion. Blackberry leaf tea serves as a remedy for digestive complaints, and tea made from the roots of blackberry brambles is used to ease the pains of childbirth.

Maple sap is an expectorant and helpful in clearing lung congestion. Maple also has compounds that improve pancreatic function.

STRAWBERRIES WITH CORN GRITS SHORTCAKES

Oteehiminani Chaakisii Pahkwesikani

SERVES 6 The coarse Pima corn grits from the Native-owned Ramona Farms (see Resources, page 291) have a robust feel and nutty flavor that only heightens the earthiness of the wild rice flour. Together, they change these shortcakes from a soft biscuit to a heartier grit cake. These shortcakes cater to gluten-free guests as well as vegetarians.

2 cups wild rice flour (see Resources, page 293)

½ cup cooked coarse Pima corn grits

1 tablespoon baking powder

1 teaspoon sea salt

¼ cup pure maple sugar (see Resources, page 291)

1 cup pecan or oat milk

1 large duck egg, lightly beaten

1 pint (2 cups) fresh strawberries, stemmed and sliced

Maple Cream (page 58), for drizzling

▸ Preheat the oven to 350°F. Line a 6-cup muffin tin with parchment liners or spray with nonstick cooking spray.

▸ Whisk together the rice flour, corn grits, baking powder, salt, and maple sugar in a large bowl. Make a well in the center.

▸ Pour the pecan milk and egg into the well, then stir the ingredients until they are smooth but not overmixed.

▸ Divide the batter among the prepared muffin cups. Bake the shortcakes for 30 minutes, or until golden brown. Allow the shortcakes to cool in the pan for 15 minutes before serving.

▸ Place the shortcakes on plates and spoon the sliced strawberries over the shortcakes. Drizzle each with some maple cream for a lightly sweet finish to a summer meal. These shortcakes are also delicious with a dollop of whipped coconut cream.

BERRY SORBET

Miinaki

SERVES 4 If you have soft or bruised blackberries, raspberries, or strawberries not quite pretty enough to serve in a salad or on a shortcake, you do not have to throw them out. Those fresh yet imperfect berries are perfect to use in sauces and in this vivid sorbet. I prefer the intensity of fresh fruit, but you can certainly use frozen. The sumac provides just the right amount of acidity here to balance the sweetness—and with only three ingredients and no churning, what could be easier?

2 cups mixed berries, such as blackberries, raspberries, and strawberries, fresh or frozen

¼ cup pure maple syrup

1 teaspoon ground sumac

▸ Bring the berries, maple syrup, and sumac to a simmer in a medium saucepan over low heat, stirring frequently. Once the berries become soft and lightly bubbly, after 5 to 7 minutes, transfer them to a blender and purée until thick and smooth.

▸ Pour the berries into a metal bowl or baking pan and cover with plastic wrap, making sure the plastic wrap touches the surface of the mixture. Freeze for at least 8 hours or overnight.

▸ When you are ready to serve, scoop the sorbet into ice-cream dishes and enjoy.

FLOATING DUCK ISLANDS WITH BERRIES AND SQUASH CREAM

Tanokootenwi Siisiipe'a Menetheehi Miinaki Aapikooni

SERVES 6 During an early-summer trip to Savannah, Georgia, I enjoyed a multicourse meal at a neighborhood bistro called Flora and Fauna. The final course was a dessert of floating islands in a crème anglaise with sliced fresh peaches. It was heavenly, and it stirred my creative juices into figuring out how to adapt this striking and delicate dish with native ingredients and no dairy. Here is the airy, cloudlike result. It will wow your guests with its beauty and color, and it will surprise with its lightness.

FOR THE ISLANDS

8 large duck egg whites, at room temperature

5 tablespoons pure maple sugar

¼ teaspoon cream of tartar

FOR THE BERRY SAUCE

2 cups mixed berries, such as blackberries, blueberries, and raspberries

¼ cup pure maple syrup

1 teaspoon blue cornmeal

½ cup squash purée (see page 118), for drizzling

1 cup mixed fresh berries, such as blackberries, blueberries, and raspberries for garnish

▶ Preheat the oven to 350°F. Line a baking sheet with parchment paper.

▶ Beat the egg whites in the bowl of a stand mixer fitted with the whisk attachment on high speed. Slowly add the maple sugar and then the cream of tartar, continuing to beat the egg whites until stiff peaks form.

▶ Using a large ice-cream scoop, scoop the egg white mixture and set the scoops about 2 inches apart on the prepared baking sheet. Bake the meringues for 10 to 15 minutes, until lightly set but not dry and bronze. They should be just done, soft, and still white. Let them cool completely on the pan.

▶ While the meringues bake and cool, stir together the mixed berries and maple syrup in a medium saucepan over low heat. Once the berries begin to simmer and break down, after 5 to 7 minutes, stir in the blue cornmeal and allow the sauce to thicken for 3 to 5 minutes more. Strain the sauce through a fine-mesh sieve into a bowl and cool.

▶ On the bottom of 6 dessert plates, spoon and swirl 3 to 4 tablespoons of the berry sauce to create a pool, then set a meringue in the center of each pool. Place a few fresh berries around each meringue, then drizzle with the squash purée and serve.

ALWAYS WELCOME AT INTERTRIBAL FRIENDSHIP HOUSE

My nephew Michael Andrews paused before beating on the drum again. "If you're not familiar with round dancing, just walk with your left foot and follow with your right foot clockwise. The family will come out and support you."

He tapped out a soft beat to get some of the more reluctant dancers moving. Teenagers in traditional dress—ribbon and jingle skirts, carrying dance sticks—moved around the tile floor to encourage guests and elders to join. "One thing about our small community here in the Bay Area," Michael continued, "is all of us, these folks, are related one way or another when we made relations a long time ago with the original Relocation Act."

On any given Wednesday night in Fruitvale, a community gathering takes place. There is a shared potluck dinner and to-go boxes of fresh produce provided to elders and those who need assistance. Michael leads the youth drumming program at the Intertribal Friendship House (IFH), which celebrated its seventieth anniversary in January 2025.

IFH was founded at the downtown YMCA building by California Natives who witnessed thousands of Natives from other parts of the country pour into Oakland beginning in the mid-1950s. The majority of those arriving had been given only a one-way bus ticket and the promise of jobs. Some wore the traditional attire of their tribes when they arrived, and most had no money and no training in the jobs that were available, even if those employers were willing to hire Native peoples. Absorbing more than a hundred different tribal bands and Indigenous communities was like welcoming immigrants from more than a hundred different countries, all with distinct languages, customs, traditions, and practices.

The American Friends Service Committee, which had been working with Native communities in New Mexico, eventually purchased the building on International Boulevard and donated it to Oakland's Native community, and it is where the IFH continues to provide food and health workshops, traditional education in drum and dance, native beading, and languages. Between the 1950s and 1990s, IFH focused more on social services. Now, people want to reconnect with their cultures.

All along the walls of IFH are pictures taken by a Navajo photographer of the descendants of those original relocation families. My uncle Bill's photo hangs on the Wall of Heroes. His widow, Carol Wahpepah, retired in 2024 after twenty years of serving as IFH's executive director. Before coming to IFH, she led the Indian Education Center at the American Indian Child Resource Center for two decades. When I was a kid, Bill and Carol let me cook in their kitchen. When I was getting started in catering, they and Sarah Poncho invited me to cook from the IFH kitchens and use produce grown in the garden beds surrounding the courtyard, where IFH grows tobacco, sweetgrass, peppers, tomatoes, and strawberries. IFH has been a constant for me.

The Wahpepah family traveled to the 148th annual Ponca Powwow in August 2024, where they participated in War Dance contests.

Greens, Tubers, and Seeds
Otaatopakooni, Ohpeniyeeki, Miinekaanani

As we rebuild our relationship to the land, its plants and animals, and retrain our palates away from sugar and salt and toward the true whole foods that are literally right under our noses, we will begin to look at our world with compassion and gratitude. No longer will that field of grass be one we drive past, but rather it will be a potential buffet of beneficial greens and fungi. Those dandelions we consider pesky weeds actually are delicious and healthful additions to salads and stocks. By thinking about and experiencing our food outside of the produce aisle of a grocery store or packaged for our convenience, we will begin to slow down and take notice. Our bodies and minds will readjust to seasonal rhythms as they are designed to do. And maybe we will not be so hungry—physically, spiritually, emotionally—because we have filled our bellies with plants, nuts, seeds, and fruits that transform us from the inside out.

You do not have to live on a farm to be in harmony with Creation. It does help to plant a garden, even in containers on your apartment balcony or in a window that gets direct sun. A forage in the middle of a vacant piece of land in Shawnee, Oklahoma, uncovered true morels just ready to be panfried. One walk through a city park in Minneapolis revealed a veritable smorgasbord of nettles, rosehips, herbs, and edible flowers that not only taste amazing right from the ground but also offer many healing properties. Pharmaceutical companies understand this, because their research relies on the curative aspects of plants to develop medicines that we pay exorbitant amounts for that are right there in our gardens for us to enjoy.

FIDDLEHEAD SALAD WITH SUNFLOWER VINAIGRETTE

Otaatopakooni Peeskoneiihi

SERVES 4 The coiled green stalks of fiddlehead ferns (*Matteuccia struthiopteris*) rising from the mossy forest floor possess an alien-looking, almost cartoonish quality, but they make a luscious spring salad. They have a vegetal flavor akin to green beans or broccoli that captures the terroir of wherever they are harvested.

½ pound fresh fiddleheads

1 pound spring mix lettuce

½ cup fresh gooseberries or cranberries

½ cup fresh blackberries

1 recipe Sunflower Vinaigrette (recipe follows)

¼ cup toasted sunflower seeds (see page 154), for garnish

▸ Fill a large metal bowl with ice for an ice bath. Line a baking sheet with paper towels.

▸ Soak the fiddleheads in clean water to cover, then drain them a couple times to make sure any dirt caught in their coils has washed away.

▸ Fill a pot with salted water and bring to a boil. Plunge the fiddleheads into the boiling water for 3 to 4 minutes, until the plant turns greener than it already is. Remove the fiddleheads with a slotted spoon and immediately plunge them into the ice bath to stop the cooking. Drain them on the prepared baking sheet.

▸ Pile the spring mix, gooseberries, blackberries, and fiddleheads in a large bowl and toss with the sunflower vinaigrette. Top with the crunchy sunflower seeds and serve.

SUNFLOWER VINAIGRETTE

MAKES 1 CUP

¼ cup sunflower oil

¼ cup cider vinegar

¼ cup olive oil

3 tablespoons agave syrup

1 teaspoon sea salt

▸ Combine the sunflower oil, vinegar, oil, agave syrup, and salt in a blender and pulse to emulsify the vinaigrette.

▸ Transfer the mixture to an airtight container and keep refrigerated until ready to use or for up to 2 weeks.

TIP

This vinaigrette is also a zesty marinade for meats and roasted root vegetables.

SPRING SALAD WITH MINER'S LETTUCE, EDIBLE FLOWERS, AND VINAIGRETTE

Aamenookamiiki Otaatopakooni Peeskoneiihi

SERVES 4 We grow miner's lettuce (*Claytonia perfoliata*) at Heron Shadow farm for our spring menu. It is a flowering herb native to the West Coast's coastal mountain areas and tastes a bit like fresh asparagus. The lettuce leaves look like lily pads or hearts, which makes sense because they are one of the richest plant sources for heart-healthy omega-3 fatty acids. The edible flowers give this spring salad a decidedly feminine quality.

¼ cup cider vinegar

¼ cup olive oil

¼ cup pure maple syrup

⅛ teaspoon sea salt

1 pound miner's lettuce

½ cup edible spring flowers, such as violets and pansies

▸ Whisk the vinegar, oil, maple syrup, and salt in a large bowl until they have coalesced into a glossy, fragrant vinaigrette.

▸ Toss the lettuce and edible flowers into the vinaigrette, making sure that every leaf and petal shines. Divide the spring salad among 4 plates and serve.

GOOD MEDICINE

Many people today consider the clusters of miner's lettuce that grow with abandon to be a weed, but Native Americans have long prized it for its astringent qualities that could quell the sting of an insect or calm irritated skin. They ate it raw or cooked, and it was known to cure headaches and sleeplessness. Science has proven that the lettuce's high magnesium levels help with fatigue, and that the leaves and stems are a natural source of lithium, which helps stabilize moods.

WINTER SALAD WITH DANDELION GREENS AND MAPLE-SUMAC VINAIGRETTE

Otaatopakooni Thiithapaakwamisi-Maakomisi

SERVES 4 For some reason, we stop eating salads once the weather turns colder, seemingly reserving these delicious greens only for longer days. Although the berries and flowers may have gone dormant, our taste buds have not. What I love about this salad is that sweet summer fruits have yielded to crunchy, woodsy nuts and seeds that beckon us to come settle in. The bitter greens and pungent onion are like exclamation marks on the tongue. The smoky caramel notes of the vinaigrette pull it all together.

1 pound dandelion greens

½ cup toasted pumpkin seeds (see page 117)

¼ cup pecan halves and pieces

¼ cup walnut halves and pieces

¼ small red onion, thinly sliced

1 recipe Maple-Sumac Vinaigrette (recipe follows)

▸ Toss the dandelion greens, pumpkin seeds, pecans, walnuts, and red onion together in a large bowl. Pour over the vinaigrette and toss again to coat all the ingredients.

▸ Serve this winter salad as a side to Bison Stew (page 199) or Kickapoo Chili (page 206).

GOOD MEDICINE

Nearly every week I learn something new about how much of a superfood dandelions are. The flowers and leaves are both edible, but the leaves have filtering properties that help remove impurities and excess fluids from the body. It is as if they cleanse the body's own cleansing organs, the liver and kidneys. And because dandelion leaves help remove bloat and swelling and pack a hefty dose of calcium, they are especially essential for women who have already gone through menopause.

MAPLE-SUMAC VINAIGRETTE

MAKES 1 CUP

½ cup cider vinegar

½ cup olive oil

2 tablespoons pure maple syrup or raw honey

1 tablespoon ground sumac

▶ Whisk together the vinegar, oil, maple syrup, and sumac in a 2-cup measuring cup with a pouring spout until all the ingredients have emulsified. Enjoy on your favorite salad.

▶ Store any unused vinaigrette in an airtight container in the refrigerator for up to 2 weeks.

GOOD MEDICINE

Depending on where you live, maple syrup and wildflower honey, each specific to different regions, offer a light sweetness while also building tolerance against seasonal allergies.

TURNIP, APPLE, AND BEET SLAW

Mesiimina

SERVES 4 For an alternative to the typical cabbage slaw dripping with mayonnaise or vinegar, I offer this slaw with a shattering crunch and a subtle interplay among the five basic tastes. Beets bring the sweet taste of Mother Earth, while the turnips pick up bitter notes like a radish. The apples offer a tartness tempered by the honey and brightened by the lemon. The cranberries shine like gems of juiciness. Bring this one to your next gathering.

Juice of 1 lemon

¼ cup honey

½ teaspoon sea salt

3 beets, peeled and grated

3 turnips, peeled and grated

2 apples, such as Granny Smith, Braeburn, or McIntosh, cored, peeled, and grated

½ cup dried cranberries

▸ Whisk the lemon juice, honey, and salt in a small bowl.

▸ In a large bowl, toss together the beets, turnips, apples, and cranberries. Drizzle with the honey dressing, then toss the slaw until the dressing is distributed evenly and lightly coats everything.

▸ Cover and set the slaw in the refrigerator for at least 30 minutes, or until ready to serve as a cool, crisp side to the White Fish Tostadas (page 237).

TIP

You can grate the beets, turnips, and apples, in that order, easily if you have a food processor with a grating attachment. Otherwise, use a box grater.

WILD ONION SOUP

Saakahneehaki Nepoopii

SERVES 4 During the late winter and early spring, just before the cool yields to longer days and brighter sun, wild onions, ramps, and morels grow abundantly throughout Oklahoma. When March arrives each year, the urge to forage for the garlicky ramps takes over, and I seek the flat green leaves and the hint of red stems shooting up from still-brown grasses. The honeycombed morel can be harder to find within wooded areas, so I substitute chaga powder. Chaga is an especially important mushroom that grows primarily on birch trees. It is a fantastic addition to all kinds of recipes, as it has a mild flavor that lends itself well to both sweet and savory dishes. Chaga is easy to use: Simply powder the bark-like mushroom and add it by the teaspoon.

- 2 teaspoons olive oil
- 1 pound wild onions or ramps, greens attached, chopped to equal 2 cups
- 1 teaspoon sea salt
- ½ teaspoon freshly ground black pepper
- 1 garlic clove, coarsely chopped
- 1 teaspoon chaga mushroom powder
- 2 cups Vegetable Stock (page 97)

▶ Heat the oil in a Dutch oven over medium heat. Stir in the onions, sprinkle with the salt and pepper, and cook, stirring frequently, for 15 minutes, or until the onions are translucent and only beginning to brown. Stir in the garlic and mushroom powder and cook for another minute to release their fragrance.

▶ Add the vegetable stock and 1 cup water and bring to a boil. Cover, reduce the heat to low, and simmer for 30 minutes, until all of the flavors have come together and the soup has slightly thickened.

▶ Serve this warm, fragrant soup with Sweet Blue Cornbread (page 81) to crumble into the bowl.

▶ Store any leftovers in an airtight container in the refrigerator for up to 3 days.

Note

If you live in an area where wild onions, such as ramps, nodding onions, textile onions, and even field garlic are plentiful, you can substitute them for store-bought onions in any recipe.

GOOD MEDICINE

Chaga is an excellent anti-inflammatory, and it has been used to fight cancer, lower blood pressure, and will help to protect the brain from neurodegeneration. Chaga mushroom powder is readily available through online sources and at natural and health food stores nationwide.

All types of onions will help lower blood pressure and bad cholesterol. In addition, onions will help relieve lung and sinus congestion.

RAINBOW POTATO WEDGES WITH SMOKED CEDAR SALT

Ohpeniyeeki Pahteewi Sekwaakwa Ihskopahaakani

SERVES 4 TO 6 Potatoes grew wild throughout the Americas, but evidence suggests that a single area in Peru is where Indigenous peoples living high in the Andes figured out how to cultivate potatoes more than seven thousand years ago. (They also knew how to freeze-dry and powder potatoes for flour.) Potatoes are an easily portable food that is low in fat and high in carbohydrates, potassium, and fiber. So, when they are not fried, they are part of a healthy diet—as they have been for millennia. This recipe represents one of my favorite ways to prepare potatoes, with a little sweetness, a little smokiness, and a lot of color.

1 pound rainbow potatoes, cut into wedges

¼ cup pure maple syrup

2 tablespoons olive oil

2 tablespoons smoked cedar salt (see Resources, page 291)

▸ Preheat the oven to 425°F.

▸ Scatter the potatoes in a single layer on a baking sheet.

▸ Stir together the maple syrup and oil in a bowl and pour it over the potatoes. Sprinkle the smoked salt evenly over the potatoes, then toss to coat them all over.

▸ Roast the potatoes for 30 minutes, or until they are golden brown and fork-tender.

▸ Serve them alongside the Bison Ribs with Blueberry Barbecue Sauce (page 205).

SWEET POTATO AND SMOKED HIBISCUS TAQUITOS WITH TOMATILLO SALSA AND HIBISCUS SAUCE

Ihskopihpeniiya Pahteewi Peeskoneiihi Mekohi Ithakahaakanaapowi

SERVES 6 Mashed, baked, or fried, sweet potatoes have a luscious fruity-floral quality that pairs well with the spices and citrus notes of the subtropics in this dish, which is both vegetarian and packed with layers of natural immunity boosters. It makes a beautiful presentation with shades of orange, bright green, and a deep pink-red on the plate. The crackle and musky flavor of the corn tortilla yields to a soft and sweet, lightly smoky filling—a satisfying combination.

2 large sweet potatoes

2 tablespoons olive oil

2 teaspoons sea salt

¼ cup dried hibiscus flowers

1 cup sunflower oil

6 Native Corn Tortillas (page 84)

1 recipe Tomatillo Salsa (recipe follows), for serving

1 recipe Hibiscus Sauce (recipe follows), for serving

Note

For a nonvegetarian version of this dish, fold 6 ounces hot-smoked salmon into the sweet potato–smoked hibiscus mixture.

▶ Preheat the oven to 350°F.

▶ Rub the sweet potatoes with the olive oil and 1 teaspoon of the salt. Place the sweet potatoes on a baking sheet and bake for 45 minutes, or until they are fork-tender.

▶ Meanwhile, bring 2 cups water to a boil in a small saucepan. Add the hibiscus flowers and cook over medium heat until the flowers soften, about 10 minutes. Drain the flowers, then spread them out on a baking sheet.

▶ On another baking sheet, place ½ cup soaked mesquite wood chips.

▶ When the sweet potatoes come out of the oven, allow them to cool until comfortable to handle.

▶ Put both the flowers and wood chips into the oven and roast for 10 minutes so that the flowers take on the smoky essence of the mesquite.

▶ Once the sweet potatoes are cool enough to handle, scrape the flesh away from the skins into a bowl. Add the smoked hibiscus flowers and the remaining 1 teaspoon salt and mash them together.

▶ Heat the sunflower oil in a deep-sided skillet until it reaches 350°F on a candy/deep-fry thermometer.

Continued

▸ Line a plate with paper towels.

▸ Spread a heaping tablespoon of the sweet potato mixture in the center of each tortilla and roll the tortillas into tight cigars. Use toothpicks, one on each end, to hold the tortillas in place.

▸ Fry the taquitos in small batches of two at a time for 3 to 5 minutes, until golden brown all over. Drain on the prepared plate.

▸ Serve the taquitos warm with the tomatillo and hibiscus sauces for drizzling or dipping.

GOOD MEDICINE

Somewhere in Central and South America, Indigenous peoples began cultivating sweet potatoes five thousand years ago, and this storage root—it's not a tuber—has been a staple of native cuisine ever since. Orange and purple cultivars were eaten by the Taíno people throughout the Bahamas and Caribbean long before Columbus arrived and even longer before South Carolina farmers planted their seeds in the ground. Sweet potatoes, which are misnamed, as they are the root of a distinct family of morning glories, is almost the perfect food package. The "sweet" is misleading because sweet potatoes have high amounts of dietary fiber and a low glycemic index. Their high levels of B complex vitamins means they support health at the most basic levels, from developing red blood cells to brain development.

TOMATILLO SALSA

MAKES 3 CUPS

6 tomatillos, brown skin removed, halved

8 small white onions, quartered

1 jalapeño pepper, stemmed and seeded

1 garlic clove

¼ cup roughly chopped fresh cilantro

2 tablespoons agave syrup

1 teaspoon sea salt

½ teaspoon ground cumin

▸ Preheat the oven to 350°F.

▸ Place the tomatillos, cut-sides down, in a roasting pan and scatter around the onions, jalapeño, and garlic. Roast the tomatillos for 10 to 12 minutes, until they are soft. Allow them to cool slightly.

▸ Transfer the roasted tomatillos and aromatics to a blender. Add the cilantro, agave syrup, salt, and cumin, then blend until smooth.

▸ Serve chilled or at room temperature. This salsa is a zingy condiment and is a light, bright dip for homemade tortilla chips (see page 88).

▸ Store any leftovers in an airtight container in the refrigerator for up to 3 weeks.

HIBISCUS SAUCE

MAKES 2 CUPS

1 cup dried hibiscus flowers

¼ cup pure maple syrup

1 tablespoon cornstarch

▸ Bring the hibiscus flowers and 1 cup water to a boil in a medium saucepan over medium heat. Cook for 5 to 7 minutes, until the flowers turn dark and soften.

▸ Drain the flowers and return the flowers to the pan. Stir in the maple syrup and cornstarch and continue cooking for about 10 minutes, until the sauce has turned thick and creamy.

▸ Serve at room temperature as a dipping sauce for the taquitos. Store any leftovers in an airtight container in the refrigerator for up to three weeks.

SWEET POTATO TOSTADAS WITH CHILI OIL AND PUMPKIN SEED CREAM

Ihskopihpeniiya Chipitiini Pemi Kaskinwiihi Miinekaanani

SERVES 4 This dish is one of our bestsellers in the restaurant because of the interplay of textures—soft, crisp, crunchy—and the layers of flavor from sweet to smoky to earthy to a little spicy heat. When you engage all of the senses with a single dish, it is much easier to eat for healing and pleasure.

1 large sweet potato

1 large russet potato

¼ cup sunflower oil

1 (8-ounce) hot-smoked salmon fillet (see Note, page 146)

3 tablespoons New Mexico chili powder

2 tablespoons smoked cedar salt (see Resources, page 196)

4 homemade tostadas (see page 88)

¼ cup pickled red onions, for serving

¼ cup Chili Oil (page 46), for serving

¼ cup Pumpkin Seed Cream (recipe follows), for serving

▸ Preheat the oven to 350°F.

▸ Roast the sweet potato and russet potato directly on the middle oven rack for 30 minutes.

▸ Let the potatoes rest.

▸ Heat the sunflower oil in a deep-sided skillet to 350°F on a candy/deep-fry thermometer. When the potatoes are cool enough to handle, quarter them and place them in the hot oil. Fry them for 2 to 4 minutes per side, until browned and the skin is crispy.

▸ Combine the potatoes, salmon, chili powder, and smoked salt in a large bowl and mash together. The mash should be chunky, where you can see pieces of potato and salmon.

▸ Spoon the potato-salmon mash equally among the 4 tostadas and top with the pickled onions, a drizzle of chili oil, and the pumpkin seed cream.

PUMPKIN SEED CREAM

MAKES 1½ CUPS

1 tomatillo, roasted (see Tip, page 121)

Small bunch of fresh cilantro roughly chopped

½ cup toasted pumpkin seeds (see page 117)

1 garlic clove, smashed

1 teaspoon sea salt

▸ Combine the tomatillo, cilantro, pumpkin seeds, garlic, salt, and ¼ cup water in a blender or food processor. Purée until the mixture has a creamy, almost mousse-like texture.

▸ Use as a sauce for the homemade tostadas or the Wild Rice Cakes (page 256).

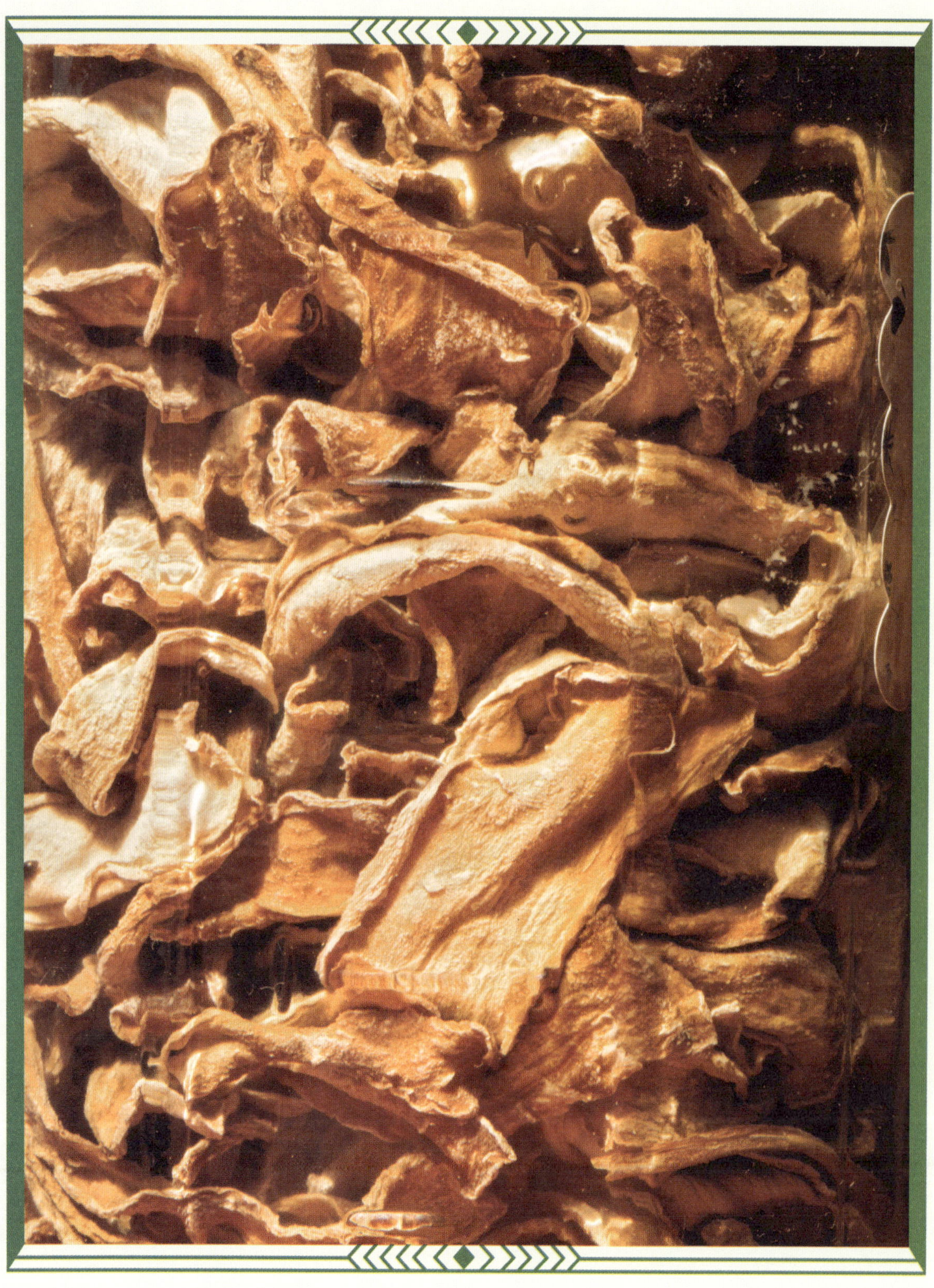

WILD NATIVE MUSHROOMS

Chipaeesiihooni Kaskinwiihi

SERVES 4 Hen of the woods (*Grifola frondosa*) or maitake mushrooms are meaty mushrooms with a naturally crunchy texture and woodsy flavor—pure umami. Brownish gray and white in color, they grow in undulating clusters near the bases of old-growth oaks and maples. They are foraged during the late summer and early autumn months of August and September. These mushrooms carry loads of vitamin D and are powerhouse immunity protectors, according to medical research.

1 recipe Tomatillo Salsa (page 183)

1 pound hen of the woods mushrooms, rinsed, dried, and broken into bite-size pieces

2 cups cooked black tepary beans (see page 43), for serving

1 recipe soft Native Corn Tortillas (page 84), for serving

1 recipe Toasted Pumpkin Seed Mole (page 188), for serving

▸ Heat the tomatillo salsa in a large saucepan or Dutch oven over low heat. Stir in the mushrooms and cook for 20 to 25 minutes, until the mushrooms have softened and the salsa has reduced and thickened.

▸ Serve the mushrooms with the black tepary beans, soft tortillas, and pumpkin seed mole as a light and deeply satisfying meal.

VARIATION

ROASTED VEGETABLES

SERVES 4 TO 6 If you do not have access to meaty mushrooms, you can substitute roasted vegetables.

1 pound winter vegetables, such as red potatoes, sweet potatoes, butternut squash, and parsnips, or summer vegetables, such as crookneck squash, carrots, zucchini, and onions

¼ cup pure maple syrup

2 tablespoons olive oil

2 tablespoons smoked cedar salt (see Resources, page 291)

▸ Preheat the oven to 375°F.

▸ Toss and coat the vegetables with the maple syrup, oil, and smoked salt in a large bowl. Arrange them in a single layer in a roasting pan or on a baking sheet.

▸ Roast the vegetables for 30 to 45 minutes, until golden brown. Serve the vegetables as in the Wild Mushroom variation.

TOASTED PUMPKIN SEED MOLE

Kaskinwiihi Miinekaanani

SERVES 4 (ABOUT 2 CUPS) This sauce, or salsa, has its roots in precolonial Mexico, during the reign of the Aztecs. It included a bitter chocolate base and was served during celebrations. Through the Spanish conquest and the transatlantic slave trade, spices, nuts, and seeds from Africa, Spain, and, later, Asia were incorporated into the moles that often still are served now, such as the mole poblano, which is thought to be the national dish of Mexico. There are multiple variations and interpretations of mole today, and this one combines the earthiness of pumpkin seeds with the bright tartness of tomatillos.

1 cup raw pumpkin seeds

2 tablespoons vegetable oil

1 teaspoon ground cumin

1 teaspoon smoked cedar salt (see Resources, page 291)

1 tomatillo, brown skin removed

½ medium white onion, quartered

2 garlic cloves

Small bunch of fresh cilantro, leaves coarsely chopped

▸ Preheat the oven to 350°F. Line a baking sheet with aluminum foil.

▸ Toss the pumpkin seeds, 1 tablespoon of the oil, the cumin, and smoked salt in a bowl. Spread the seeds in a single layer on the prepared baking sheet. Toast the seeds for 15 minutes, tossing them every 5 minutes, until they are golden brown and release a nutty, smoky aroma. Set aside to cool.

▸ Raise the oven temperature to 450°F. Line another baking sheet with aluminum foil and brush it with the remaining 1 tablespoon oil.

▸ Cut the tomatillo in half and place the halves, cut-sides down, on the prepared baking sheet. Add the onion and garlic to the pan. Roast the tomatillo, onion, and garlic for 20 minutes, or until soft and lightly caramelized.

▸ Combine the roasted tomatillo, onion, and garlic, and the pumpkin seeds, cilantro, and ½ cup water in a food processor and pulse until smooth but textured.

▸ Serve with toasted tortillas for a healthy snack or as a sauce with Roasted Rabbit (page 214), Roasted Vegetables (page 187), or roasted chicken.

FRIED MORELS

SERVES 4 Sometime during the two weeks at the end of March and the first two weeks of April, I make my way back to Shawnee, Oklahoma, where my cousin Nick Wahpepah and my nephew Ryan are my guides to hunting morels. They know of places—secret ones—right in the city between houses and businesses, where forested areas are still damp from rain and fallen leaves will cover their tracks. Morels are wrinkled fungi that grow on stems and are hollow inside. They must never be eaten raw or undercooked because they can cause a stomach upset that could be serious enough to send you to the hospital. Like other cooked mushrooms, their benefits are profound, contributing to strong immune systems and cardiovascular health.

- 1 cup sunflower oil or duck fat
- 1 pound fresh morels
- ½ cup fine white cornmeal
- 1 teaspoon sea salt
- 2 large duck eggs, lightly beaten

▶ Heat the oil in a deep-sided skillet to 325° to 350°F on a candy/deep-fry thermometer.

▶ Submerge the morels in water and swish them around to shake out any dirt hiding in their wrinkles. Dry them well. Halve the large ones (about the size of a lemon) and keep the small ones (the size of a chicken egg) whole.

▶ Line a plate with paper towels.

▶ Mix the cornmeal and salt in a pie pan or other shallow dish. Place the beaten eggs in another pie pan or other shallow dish.

▶ Dip the morels into the beaten eggs and then the cornmeal, making sure they are coated all over. Plunge the morels into the hot oil and fry them in small batches of two or three for 5 to 6 minutes, until they are golden brown and cooked through. Drain the fried morels on the prepared plate. Serve warm.

CHIA SEED PUDDING

Miinekaanani

SERVES 4 This simple three-ingredient dessert (or snack) reminds me of tapioca pudding in texture but without the heaviness. The coconut milk gives the pudding a slightly tropical taste. And the chia seeds up the health quotient because they soak up so much moisture, thickening the pudding without flour or cream, that they actually act as soluble fiber—that ever-important type of fiber that is missing from most modern diets but is essential for lowering bad cholesterol and managing blood sugar levels.

1 cup coconut milk
¼ cup chia seeds
¼ cup agave syrup

TIP

Double the deliciousness by layering the Chia Seed Pudding on top of the Chokecherry Pudding (page 154) for a beautiful color-blocked and creamy bowl of goodness. Garnish with fresh berries.

- Mix the coconut milk, chia seeds, and agave syrup in a large bowl. Cover the bowl and set it in the refrigerator for 4 hours.
- Divide the pudding among 4 clear bowls or pudding cups to show off how the seeds expand and rise to the top, creating layers.

GOOD MEDICINE

Chia are the tiny seeds of a desert plant from the mint family (*Salvia hispanica*) and are indigenous to Central America. They offer enough heart-healthy omega-3 fatty acids to reduce triglyceride levels in the body and increase bone density. Just 1 ounce of chia seeds delivers 23 percent of the recommended daily allowance of magnesium, which, among its many benefits, helps with lowering anxiety and promoting restful sleep. Because chia hold so many vitamins and minerals and are high in fiber, the seeds help with appetite management and weight loss. Chia seeds may have been the food of the warriors among Aztecs and Mayans, but considering the variety of symptoms experienced by women in midlife today, chia seeds added to oatmeal, smoothies, and other dishes may help alleviate the effects of perimenopause.

3

GAME AND FISH

Wiiyaathi Chakisii Memeethaki

Because Native Americans ate a largely plant-based diet, proteins were hunted from what was wild and local. Unlike these modern times, meat was not the center of the meal. Beef, pork, and chicken were not staples of our diets either. Rather, American bison (Bison bison), venison from deer, wild turkey, small game like rabbit, and seafood from both fresh and salt waters provided the main sources of protein depending upon where the people lived. For the Kickapoo, deer was—and is—a sacred food source. Even when we lived on the plains where bison was plentiful, deer was prized above all else. For Indigenous people in the Northeast and Southwest, the dazzling plumage of wild turkeys is used as part of ceremonial regalia to signify their importance to the tribal cultures. For the nations of the Pacific Northwest, salmon is a unifying element of their foodways and traditions.

Wild, local, and minimal—this way remains a good approach to eating. Again, though, we have to retrain our palates. That retraining involves seeking sources that are as close to wild and local as possible (e.g., grassfed) and accepting darker meats, earthier flavors, and smaller portions.

GAME AND FISH

Wiiyaathi Chakisii Memeethaki

Continued ▸

BISON STEW

Misiikwaa Nepoopii

SERVES 6 TO 8 Oakland is cold well into the early months of summer, and this stew keeps me warm inside and out. Because bison is not marbled through with fat, you need a bit of oil to caramelize it or it will be a little tough. By sautéing the vegetables until they just soften, you retain their color and texture, which gives this stew a lot of character and heartiness.

2 pounds bison stew meat

1 tablespoon sea salt

2 teaspoons freshly ground black pepper

2 tablespoons olive or sunflower oil

6 medium carrots, cut into 1-inch rounds

6 celery stalks, diced

1 small white onion, chopped

2 garlic cloves

1 cup cooked hominy (see page 43; optional)

1 bay leaf

12 cups water or Vegetable Stock (page 97)

▸ Season the bison meat with the salt and pepper.

▸ Heat the oil in a large stockpot over medium heat. Add the meat to the hot oil and brown the meat on all sides. When the stew meat is caramelized, remove it from the pot and set it aside.

▸ Add the carrots, celery, and onions to the same pot and sauté over medium heat for 4 to 6 minutes, until the vegetables soften. Stir in the garlic and cook for 1 minute more, or until the smell of the garlic blooms.

▸ Stir in the hominy (if using), add the bay leaf, and pour in the water or vegetable stock, scraping the bottom to release all those tasty brown bits. Return the meat to the pot, cover, reduce the heat to low, and cook for 30 to 45 minutes, until the meat is fork-tender.

▸ Serve hot in bowls with a warm side of cornbread or soft tortillas (see page 84).

BLUEBERRY BISON MEATBALLS WITH BLUEBERRY SAUCE

Miinaki Misiikwaa

SERVES 4 TO 6 This recipe is one of the most requested for catering events and one of the most popular starters in the restaurant, but for me, it's a comfort food that I've long made for my family. I personally love the bit of crunch from the blue cornmeal, which acts as a binder and thickener, and the sweet-smoky play between the bison and the blueberries. These are quick and easy to make for a party buffet or to serve as a main course with a side of Wild Rice Salad (page 260).

- 1 pound ground bison
- ½ teaspoon smoked cedar salt (see Resources, page 291)
- ¼ cup blue cornmeal
- 1 recipe Blueberry Sauce (page 202), for serving

TIPS

Make the blueberry sauce ahead so that the flavors ripen together.

Serve as a dipping sauce for Deer Sticks (page 221).

- Preheat the oven to 350°F. Line a baking sheet with parchment paper.
- Mix the ground bison, smoked salt, and cornmeal by hand in a medium bowl. Form the mixture into twelve 1-inch meatballs and set them on the prepared baking sheet. Let them rest for 10 minutes.
- Bake the meatballs for 30 to 35 minutes, until browned and cooked through.
- Serve warm with the blueberry sauce as a dip or a glaze.

GOOD MEDICINE

Bison is native to North America, and it is one of the best protein choices as an alternative to beef. It is naturally lower in calories and saturated fat and full of vitamins and minerals, such as B_{12} and iron to stave off anemia as well as heart-healthy omega-3 fatty acids. It draws many nutrients from a natural grass-grazing diet.

BLUEBERRY SAUCE

MAKES 2 CUPS The color of this sauce is something to behold! Is it purple or indigo or midnight blue? Whatever you name it, this versatile accompaniment lends itself to both sweet and savory dishes. The cornmeal acts as a thickener, much like cornstarch does, but adds a bit of texture and nutty taste.

1 pint (2 cups) fresh blueberries

¼ cup pure maple syrup

1 teaspoon blue cornmeal

▶ Stir together the blueberries and maple syrup in a medium saucepan over low heat. Once the blueberries begin to simmer and break down, after 5 to 7 minutes, stir in the blue cornmeal and allow the sauce to thicken for 3 to 5 minutes more. Strain the sauce through a fine-mesh sieve into a bowl. The sauce should be served warm with the meatballs but can be served warm or cool as a dipping sauce or glaze in other recipes. Store unused sauce in an airtight container in the refrigerator for up to a week.

VARIATION

BISON SALAD WITH BLUEBERRIES AND MAPLE PECANS

Misiikwaa Otaatopakooni Miinaki Pakaana

SERVES 4 TO 6

1 recipe warm Blueberry Bison Meatballs (page 201)

½ cup pecan halves

1 tablespoon pure maple syrup

¼ teaspoon sea salt

6 cups mixed lettuces and greens, such as arugula and dandelion greens

½ cup Berry Vinaigrette (page 146)

1 cup fresh blueberries, for serving

2 tablespoons popped amaranth, for garnish

▶ After the Blueberry Bison Meatballs come out of the oven, keep the oven warm at 350°F. Line a baking sheet with parchment paper.

▶ Toss the pecans with the maple syrup and salt in a medium bowl until they are thoroughly coated. Place them in an even layer on the prepared baking sheet.

▶ Bake the pecans for 12 to 15 minutes, until their color has deepened. Let them cool on the pan for 10 minutes.

▶ In the meantime, toss the lettuces and meatballs with the vinaigrette in a large bowl.

▶ Divide the salad among 4 to 6 plates, then top with the blueberries and maple pecans and then garnish with the popped amaranth. Serve immediately.

GOOD MEDICINE

There is so much spirit in wild blueberries. Their antioxidant properties are well known, making them important for moderating blood sugars and reducing inflammation. But that same nutrient concentration helps people suffering with addiction clear toxins from their bodies while also strengthening their immune systems during withdrawal. Blueberries' natural sweetness also addresses that need to supplant one addiction with another, but with healthy sugars rather than processed ones.

BISON RIBS WITH BLUEBERRY BARBECUE SAUCE

Misiikwaa Oopikai Miinaki

SERVES 4 Bison ribs are meaty and luscious, with or without sauce. But with sauce, the ribs take on a smoky sweetness that crisps into a nice bark and just screams summer. These ribs remain one of my favorites to serve on Memorial Day to honor my grandfather, who served in the military during World War II. So many Native Americans served to defend freedoms they did not even fully enjoy, and some tribes, like the Navajo, were instrumental in turning the tide in the Pacific theater.

- 2 (5-pound) slabs bison back ribs
- ¼ cup pure maple sugar (see Resources, page 291)
- 2 tablespoons plus 1 teaspoon sea salt
- 1 pint (2 cups) fresh blueberries
- 1 garlic clove, coarsely chopped

▸ Preheat the oven to 350°F. Line a baking sheet or roasting pan with aluminum foil.

▸ Rub the bison ribs with the maple sugar and 2 tablespoons of the salt. Place the ribs on the prepared baking sheet. Bake the ribs for 40 minutes, or until dark brown. Cover the ribs with aluminum foil and let them rest while you make the sauce.

▸ Bring the blueberries, garlic, the remaining 1 teaspoon salt, and 2 tablespoons water to a boil in a medium saucepan over medium heat, stirring frequently. Once the blueberries break down, after 7 to 10 minutes, continue cooking until the sauce is reduced by half and has thickened to where it coats the back of a spoon.

▸ Remove the blueberries from the heat and strain through a fine-mesh sieve into a bowl.

▸ Brush the ribs with the sauce to coat them in glossy deliciousness. Serve with more sauce on the side.

KICKAPOO CHILI

Kickapoo Nepoopii

SERVES 4 This recipe has been carried from one generation to the next in my family. It is the dish that most captures my heritage in its rich, spicy broth. The chilies impart both heat and brightness. The blue corn flour works as a thickener while also providing texture. The epazote (*Chenopodium ambrosioides*) is a powerfully fragrant and flavorful indigenous herb, sometimes called skunk weed, which is commonly found in Mexican grocery stores and farmers' markets. It is sometimes used dried, but the flavor is best when used fresh. The fresher it is, the stronger the taste of anise. Dried epazote tends toward a more citrus flavor. If you cannot find epazote, substitute oregano.

1 tablespoon vegetable oil

1 pound ground bison, at room temperature

1 large yellow onion, finely chopped

2 Anaheim chilies, stemmed, seeded, and finely chopped

1 jalapeño pepper, stemmed, seeded, and finely chopped

3 large tomatoes, cored and cut into medium dice

½ cup red chili paste

1 tablespoon blue corn flour

4 to 6 sprigs fresh epazote, stems removed and leaves finely chopped

▸ Line a plate with paper towels.

▸ Heat the oil in a large saucepan over medium heat. Crumble the bison into the pan and brown for 5 minutes without stirring. Break up the meat using a spatula and continue cooking for about 5 minutes, until there is no visible pink. Using a slotted spoon, transfer the meat to the prepared plate.

▸ In the same saucepan, sauté the onions, Anaheims, and jalapeño for 5 to 7 minutes, until tender. Stir in the tomatoes and chili paste and bring to a simmer so that the tomatoes release their juices. Sprinkle the corn flour over the tomato sauce and stir constantly for 3 minutes more, or until the sauce thickens.

▸ Return the meat to the pan, add the epazote, and reduce the heat to low. Cover the pan and simmer for 20 minutes, stirring occasionally, or until the chili has thickened and the bison is thoroughly cooked and tender.

▸ Serve hot in bowls with a square of Sweet Blue Cornbread (page 81).

GOOD MEDICINE

Epazote is a powerful anti-parasitic medicine and digestive aid.

Anaheim chilies, a member of the Capsicum genus, are high in vitamin C, vitamin A, and fiber—effective in relieving lung congestion and inflammation.

BISON ROAST WITH CHOKECHERRY RUB

Misiikwaa Katoowakimina

SERVES 4 TO 6 If you want to feed a lot of people an elegant cut of meat or make something special for someone you love, this roast speaks to the heart, especially because it is rubbed down with life-giving chokecherries. This roast pairs well with the Rainbow Potato Wedges with Smoked Cedar Salt (page 179) and the Acorn Squash with Maple and Pecans (page 116).

1 (4- to 6-pound) bison prime rib roast

2 tablespoons pure maple syrup

1 recipe Chokecherry Rub (page 211)

▸ Preheat the oven to 350°F.

▸ Rinse and pat dry the rib roast. Trim the silver skin from the roast and leave a nice cap of fat on top so that as the roast cooks, it self-tenderizes.

▸ Massage the maple syrup all over the roast's surface, then follow with a generous coating of the chokecherry rub. Pour 1½ cups water into the bottom of a roasting pan, set a roasting rack in the bottom, and place the roast on the rack. Cook until the roast has reached an internal temperature of 135°F on a meat thermometer for medium doneness and the outside is nice and crusty, about 2½ hours. If you'd like your roast well done, cook for 30 minutes longer or to an internal temperature of 170°F. Remove the roast from the oven and let it rest for at least 20 minutes, so all the juices can be reconstituted. Slice against the grain to serve.

TIP

Whether I am cooking bison, venison, or salmon, I slather proteins in pure maple syrup as a marinade before roasting, braising, or grilling. This step imparts some sweetness, acts as a binder for rubs and other seasonings, and when combined with cider vinegar or citrus, it can help tenderize a tough cut.

CHOKECHERRY RUB

MAKES 1 CUP No matter where I go, I bring chokecherry patties made by Luke Black Elk (Tetowan Lakota) with me, and I am still surprised by the number of people who are unaware of this small native berry and all the ways it can be used. The chokecherry shrubs grow most abundantly in rocky outcrops and forested areas in the upper portion of the Great Plains, around the Dakotas, Minnesota, and Wisconsin. Fresh-picked berries do not have a strong taste, but when they are ground and formed into patties and dried, an intense sour cherry flavor bursts through. They are dark like Bing cherries, but they are the size of small blueberries or huckleberries with a perfect little teardrop of a pit that is about the size of a pine nut. I use this dry rub most often on the Bison Roast (page 209), but it is equally good on Bison Ribs with Blueberry Barbecue Sauce (page 205) or on venison tenderloin.

1 chokecherry patty (see Resources, page 293)

½ cup pure maple sugar (see Resources, page 291)

1 tablespoon New Mexico chili powder

1 tablespoon onion powder

1 tablespoon garlic powder

1 teaspoon sea salt

▶ Break up and mash the chokecherry patty in a small bowl. If you have a mortar and a pestle, even better. Add the maple sugar, chili powder, onion powder, garlic powder, and salt and grind them together until you have a smooth mixture.

▶ Store in an airtight container in a cool dry place for up to 6 months.

GOOD MEDICINE

Chokecherries (*Prunus virginiana*) are powerful medicine because they increase gut health, and gut health is central to the mind-body connection and accounts for around 70 percent of our immune system response. Wojapi, a native berry sauce similar to a jam or jelly, made from chokecherries, can help soothe a cough because it has antispasmodic properties. Like other deeply colored berries, chokecherries are rich in antioxidants and have anti-inflammatory properties. Chokecherries are similar to black cherries (*Prunus serotina*) and both are members of the Rosaceae (rose) family.

BISON TACOS

Misiikwaa Taakohaki

SERVES 6 If you do not have Chokecherry Rub (page 211), the rub mixture in this recipe is an easy and flavorful go-to for most meats, and the maple syrup tenderizes as well as creates a caramelized coating. The crisp, cool salsa complements the rich, unctuous character of the shredded bison. This recipe also can be doubled and tripled to feed a crowd.

1 pound boneless bison chuck roast

3 garlic cloves, coarsely chopped

2 tablespoons pure maple syrup

2 tablespoons sea salt

1 recipe soft Native Corn Tortillas (page 84) or homemade tostadas (see page 88)

1 recipe Green Chili Salsa (page 121)

Small bunch of fresh cilantro, coarsely chopped

½ cup pickled red onions

- Preheat the oven to 350°F.
- Rinse and pat dry the roast.
- Mix together the garlic, maple syrup, and salt in a small bowl.
- Massage the surface of the roast with the maple rub. Place the roast in a deep baking pan or roasting pan. Roast for 1½ hours, or until the internal temperature is 135°F on a meat thermometer and the meat is tender.
- Using 2 forks or your hands, shred the roast into bite-size pieces in the pan. Load up 6 tortillas with the shredded meat and top with some of the chili salsa, cilantro, and pickled onions. Serve immediately.

CHEYENNE RIVER STEAK

Misiikwaa

SERVES 4 This bison steak mirrors the classic American chophouse meal. It is sourced from the Cheyenne River Lakota, who raise, harvest, and process their meats in South Dakota, where bison once freely roamed the Great Plains. The Lakota have one of the largest herds of tribally owned and managed bison.

- 4 (12-ounce) bison steaks
- 12 garlic cloves, finely chopped
- ¼ cup dried rosemary
- 2 tablespoons dried thyme
- 1 tablespoon sea salt
- 2 teaspoons freshly ground black pepper
- ½ cup bison fat or unsalted butter

▸ Rinse and pat dry the steaks. Allow them to rest and come to room temperature.

▸ Combine the garlic, rosemary, thyme, salt, and pepper in a medium bowl.

▸ When you are ready to cook, press the garlic mixture all over the top and bottom of the steaks.

▸ Heat a large cast-iron skillet or grill pan over medium heat. Add the bison fat and let it melt. If you need to work in batches of 1 or 2 steaks at a time, use 2 to 3 tablespoons of the fat per steak.

▸ Sear the steak on one side for 5 to 6 minutes, then flip the steak to the other side. Spoon the fat over the steak as it cooks for 5 to 6 minutes more, until the internal temperature on a meat thermometer reaches 135°F for rare or 140°F for medium.

▸ Serve with Wild Rice Salad (page 260) or Rainbow Potato Wedges with Smoked Cedar Salt (page 179).

ROASTED RABBIT, THREE WAYS

Mehsweeha

SERVES 4 The next three recipes stem from this one for roasted rabbit. Rabbit cooks best when it is slowly braised or roasted because it is a lean meat with not a lot of fat to tenderize it. Although rabbit is often compared with chicken in terms of flavor, rabbit is distinct, with a mild sweetness and subtle richness.

- 1 (1- to 2-pound) rabbit
- 2 tablespoons pure maple syrup
- 1 yellow onion, quartered
- 3 garlic cloves
- 1 dried New Mexico chili

- Preheat the oven to 350°F.
- Rinse and pat dry the rabbit and slather it with the maple syrup. Place the rabbit in a roasting pan with the onions, garlic, New Mexico chili, and 1 cup water.
- Roast the rabbit for 1½ hours, or until all the juices run clear and the internal temperature is 160°F on a meat thermometer.
- Remove the chili, then stem and seed it. Blend the chili, roasted onion, roasted garlic, and 1 cup water in a blender to create a red chili sauce.
- Pour the sauce over the rabbit, then shred the rabbit, being careful to remove all the bones.
- Roasted rabbit makes a wonderful main dish on its own or in one of the three dishes that follow.

GOOD MEDICINE

New Mexico chilies were cultivated by Puebloan cultures for hundreds of years. The cultivar that we use today was developed around 1913. The pepper grows from green to red and is large, with a thin, glossy skin. It registers between 700 and 1,400 on the Scoville heat unit scale.

The capsaicin in chilies is what gives them their heat, and it is also the ingredient in pain relief gels that alleviates joint tenderness and inflammation. Eating chilies also relieves joint pain as well as helps with weight loss because they "fire up" metabolism.

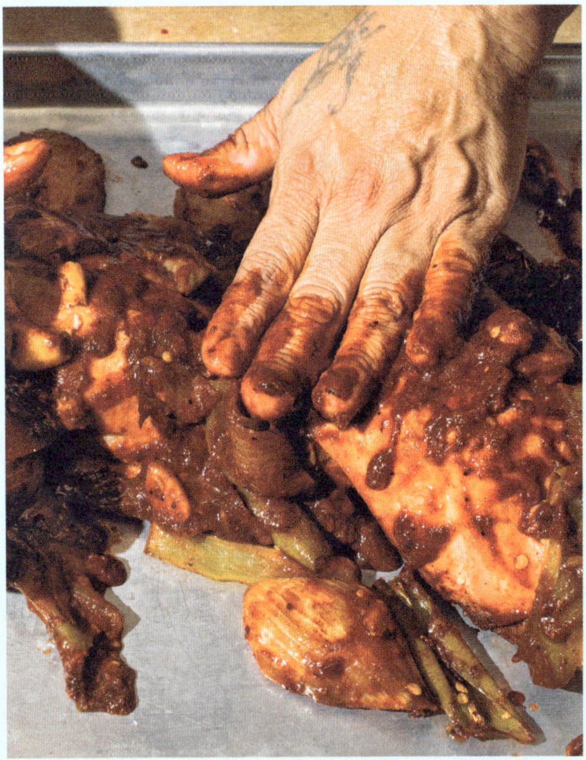

RABBIT POZOLE

SERVES 4

1 recipe Roasted Rabbit (page 214), shredded

1 cup dried white hominy

3 tablespoons dried Mexican oregano

1 teaspoon ground cumin

▸ Combine the shredded rabbit, dried hominy, oregano, cumin, and 8 cups water in a large stockpot over low heat. Cook for 3 to 4 hours, until the hominy is soft.

▸ Serve warm with Roasted Squash Blossom Cornbread (page 119).

RABBIT TAMALES

MAKES 12 TO 16

1 cup duck fat

4 cups blue corn masa harina

2 teaspoons sea salt

3 to 4 cups Vegetable Stock (page 97)

12 to 16 corn husks

1 recipe Roasted Rabbit (page 214), shredded

1 recipe Green Chili Salsa (page 121)

▸ Whip the duck fat in a large bowl with a hand mixer on medium-high speed until it is light and fluffy. Add the masa harina and salt, then mix together until you get a good dough started.

▸ Slowly add the stock and continue to mix the dough by hand until you get a thick, spreadable dough. Cover the dough with a clean kitchen towel and set aside at room temperature.

▸ Soak the corn husks in warm water for 30 minutes.

▸ Fill a large stockpot with about 2 inches of water, and bring the water to a simmer over medium heat.

▸ Working with one husk at a time, pat dry the husk, then spread the masa dough about ½ inch thick across the husk, leaving ¼ inch around the edges. Scoop 2 tablespoons of the shredded rabbit and place it in the center of the husk.

▸ Fold the sides, bottom, and top over one another to create a pouch, then tie a strip of corn husk around the tamale to hold it in place. Repeat this process until you are out of masa. (Reserve any leftover rabbit for tacos, see page 219.)

▸ Pack the tamales upright and tightly together in a steamer basket and place the steamer basket in the pot of simmering water. Cover and steam the tamales for 1 hour.

▸ Remove the tamales from the husks and serve with drizzles of salsa.

Notes

You can use the broth created from roasting the rabbit for the stock called for in this recipe. If there is not enough for 3 to 4 cups, then use vegetable stock for the remainder.

You can use yellow or white corn masa harina in place of the blue corn masa harina.

RABBIT TACOS

MAKES 8 TO 10 TACOS

1 recipe Roasted Rabbit (page 214), shredded

8 to 10 Native Corn Tortillas (page 84)

1 recipe Green Chili Salsa (page 121)

½ cup pickled red onions

1 jalapeno, sliced

¼ cup chopped cilantro

▸ Pile the shredded rabbit on each tortilla, along with a generous drizzle of green chili salsa and about a tablespoon of picked red onions. Top with the jalapenos and cilantro. Serve and enjoy.

DEER STICKS WITH CHOKECHERRY-AGAVE DIPPING SAUCE

Peesekithi'a Katoowakimina-Thiithapaakwamisi

SERVES 4 My Oklahoma relatives are avid hunters, and we often ate venison during the fall and winter months. Deer meat is deep ruby red with little fat. Its slight gaminess comes from the diet of the deer, the combination of grasses, leaves, shrubs, berries, bark, and acorns the deer ate. This enriches the meat with lots of life-giving vitamins and minerals. These deer sticks are reminiscent of kebabs and make wonderful appetizers or snacks, or can be served as part of an Indigenous Food Board (see page 242) or alongside a Strawberry-Sumac Salad with Maple-Sage Vinaigrette (page 149).

- 1 (3-pound) venison tenderloin
- 2 tablespoons pure maple syrup
- 2 teaspoons sea salt
- 1 recipe Chokecherry-Agave Dipping Sauce (page 222) for serving

TIP

Depending on how fresh the venison is, you may want to soak it in cold water for 20 to 30 minutes to remove any excess blood.

▸ Soak 8 to 10 bamboo skewers in warm water for at least 30 minutes.

▸ Heat a grill to 400°F. Rub olive or vegetable oil on the clean grate.

▸ Rinse and pat dry the tenderloin. Trim the silver skin, then cut the tenderloin into 1-inch chunks. Toss the chunks with the maple syrup and salt in a large bowl.

▸ Thread 4 to 6 venison chunks onto each bamboo skewer. Place the skewers on the grill and cook the chunks for 3 to 4 minutes on each side, until cooked through and lightly caramelized. Serve warm with the chokecherry-agave sauce.

CHOKECHERRY-AGAVE DIPPING SAUCE

MAKES 3 CUPS *Prunus virginiana*, chokecherry, is one of the most important indigenous fruits across Turtle Island. They are the fruit of a common shrub that forms dense thickets on the edges of forests and on the prairies of the Great Plains. Once the tight red berries ripen in late summer and early fall, chokecherries turn a deep maroon or plum color and taste sweet. Picked any earlier and they are bitter. This sauce complements both sweet and savory dishes, as a drizzle over Sweet Bue Cornbread (page 81) or as a glaze for Bison Ribs (page 205) and Deer Sticks (page 221).

2 cups ripe chokecherries

1 cup agave syrup

▸ Bring the chokecherries, agave syrup, and 1 cup water to a simmer in a large saucepan over low heat, stirring frequently. Cook for 30 minutes, or until the sauce has thickened and the chokecherry pits have fallen to the bottom of the pan.

▸ Strain the sauce through a fine-mesh sieve into a medium bowl. If not using immediately, store in an airtight container in the refrigerator for up to 1 week.

MAPLE-ROASTED TURKEY WINGS

Thiithapaakwamisi Peneewa

SERVES 4 According to research, Native Americans domesticated turkeys more than eight hundred years ago, but they still had their colorful plumage, dark meat, and lots of flavor—not like the colorless, bland birds found in industrial operations today. Wild turkeys, however, have that rich flavor because, unlike industrial birds, they are active and fly, which also means their wings are bigger and meatier.

- 4 wild turkey wings
- 3 garlic cloves, minced
- ½ cup pure maple syrup (see Note)
- 1 teaspoon ground sumac
- 1 teaspoon sea salt

▸ Preheat the oven to 350°F. Line a baking sheet with parchment paper.

▸ Rinse and pat dry the turkey wings. Stir the garlic, maple syrup, sumac, and salt together in a small bowl. Brush the syrup mixture all over the turkey wings.

▸ Place the wings on the prepared baking sheet. Bake the wings for 1 hour, or until golden brown and the internal temperature of the meat registers 165°F on a meat thermometer.

VENISON WILD RICE SOUP

Peesekithi'a Manoomini Nepoopii

SERVES 6 TO 8 With tender venison and toasty rice, this soup tastes like a hug. Served alongside Corn Pancakes with Wild Onions (page 77), this soup makes a most comforting meal on a cold night or a gray afternoon. Your spirits will be uplifted with all the goodness in the broth from the vegetables and rice.

- 2 pounds venison stew meat
- 1 tablespoon sea salt
- 2 teaspoons freshly ground black pepper
- 2 tablespoons olive or sunflower oil
- 6 medium carrots, cut into 1-inch rounds
- 6 celery stalks, diced
- 1 small white onion, coarsely chopped
- 2 garlic cloves
- ½ cup wild rice, cooked according to package instructions

▸ Season the venison stew meat with the salt and pepper in a large bowl.

▸ Heat the oil in a large stockpot over medium heat. Add the venison and brown the meat on all sides. When the meat is caramelized, remove it from the pot and set it aside.

▸ Add the carrots, celery, and onions to the same pot and sauté over medium heat for 4 to 6 minutes, until the vegetables soften. Stir in the garlic and cook for 1 minute more, or until the smell of the garlic blooms.

▸ Stir in the wild rice and 8 cups water, scraping the bottom to release all those tasty brown bits. Return the meat to the pot, cover, and reduce the heat to low. Cook for 30 to 45 minutes, until the meat is fork-tender. Serve hot.

▸ Store any leftover soup in an airtight container in the refrigerator for up to 4 days.

Note

To add extra layers of flavor, substitute Vegetable Stock (page 97) for the water in this recipe.

MAPLE-MARINATED VENISON MUSHROOM BITES

Thiithapaakwamisi Peesekithi'a Chipaeesiihooni

MAKES 10 TO 12 Anytime these little bites are on our catering table—which is not often because the chanterelles appear for such a short time each year and foragers pounce on them—they make a beautiful presentation. The textures complement one another, as do the flavors—the richer, more intense deer meat up against the mild fruitiness of the mushrooms.

- 1 (1-pound) venison tenderloin
- 3 tablespoons pure maple syrup
- ¼ teaspoon sea salt
- 10 to 12 chanterelle mushrooms

▸ Rinse and pat dry the tenderloin. Trim the silver skin, then cut the venison into 1-inch cubes. Toss the cubes with the maple syrup and salt in a large bowl. Cover the bowl and let the cubes marinate overnight in the refrigerator.

▸ Soak 10 to 12 small bamboo skewers in warm water for at least 30 minutes.

▸ Heat a grill to 400°F. Rub olive or vegetable oil on the clean grate.

▸ Wipe the mushrooms with a clean towel to remove any debris. Remove the venison from the refrigerator. Thread 3 venison cubes and one mushroom onto each skewer.

▸ Place the skewers on the grill and cook for 3 to 4 minutes on each side, until the venison is golden brown and caramelized. Serve immediately.

TIP

If you do not want to fire up a grill, these bites bake just as well in a preheated 400°F oven. Just line a baking sheet with parchment paper and bake the bites for 15 to 20 minutes, until the venison is golden brown.

HUNTING CHANTERELLES

Foragers covet the brief window between July and October when golden chanterelles push through the moist earth after a nice rain. (In California, that window is September through November.) They grow in groups, so if you find one, you probably will find more in woodsy areas that get partial sunlight. Their delicate frilly appearance belies a strong, meaty texture with a bright flavor, which is different from muskier varieties of mushrooms.

VENISON OR TURKEY MEATBALLS

Peesekithi'a or Peneewa

MAKES 24 Venison and turkey lend themselves to more fall-ish flavors, as do the cranberries in this recipe. These meatballs go well with several dishes in this book, including salads. I usually make a batch, then freeze them to throw into a stew or to reheat them for a protein-forward snack or as a starter ahead of the main meal.

1 pound ground venison or ground wild turkey

¼ cup dried cranberries

3 tablespoons cornmeal

1 teaspoon sea salt

▸ Preheat the oven to 350°F. Line a baking sheet with parchment paper.

▸ Mix the ground meat, cranberries, cornmeal, and salt by hand in a large bowl. Shape the meat into 1-inch meatballs and set them about ½ inch apart on the prepared baking sheet.

▸ Bake the meatballs for 15 minutes, or until they are golden brown all over and cooked through. Serve with Hand-Harvested Wild Rice Pilaf (page 259) or Wild Rice Salad (page 260).

SMOKED TURKEY SOUP WITH WILD RICE DUMPLINGS

Pahteewi Peneewa Manoomini Nepoopii

SERVES 6 TO 8 If there is a Native American version of chicken and dumplings, this recipe comes close. But with wild rice flour, the dumplings are lighter in density, nuttier in flavor, with a touch more texture with bits of ground rice. So, the dumplings are more akin to matzo balls. This is a simple weeknight soup to make, especially with leftover turkey, and the dumplings can be made ahead.

- 2 tablespoons olive oil
- 2 pounds smoked wild turkey, cubed
- 1 medium white onion, diced
- 4 carrots, diced
- 4 celery stalks, diced
- 2 teaspoons sea salt
- 1 cup ground wild rice (see Tip)
- ½ cup wild rice flour (see Resources, page 293)
- 1 large egg yolk
- 1 teaspoon baking powder

▸ Heat the oil in a large stockpot over medium heat. Add the smoked turkey, onions, carrots, and celery to the pot and sauté for 4 to 6 minutes, until the vegetables soften. Pour in 8 cups water, scrape up the tasty bits, and bring to a boil.

▸ Mix the ground rice, rice flour, egg yolk, and baking powder in a bowl to create a thick dough. Form 2-inch balls from the dough and drop the dumplings into the boiling soup.

▸ Continue cooking for 20 minutes, or until the dumplings have floated to the top and are cooked through. Ladle into bowls and serve hot.

▸ Store any leftover soup in an airtight container in the refrigerator for up to 3 days.

TIP

To grind wild rice: Rinse the wild rice until the water runs clear. Spread the rice in a single layer on a baking sheet, and dry the rice in a 170°F oven for about 20 minutes, until it is completely dry. Allow the rice to cool to room temperature.

Grind the rice in a food processor, blender, or coffee grinder in ¼ cup to ½ cup batches until it resembles a fine meal. Sift through a fine-mesh sieve into a bowl or onto a plate. Whatever is caught in the sieve, pour back into the grinder and keep repeating the process until all of the wild rice has been transformed into rice meal.

CATFISH STEW

Myaanaweekwaapowi Nepoopii

SERVES 6 TO 8 One dish that has sustained my Oklahoma family is this catfish stew. Every time my cousins go fishing and bring back one of these big, barbed fish, there is a feast with enough meat to make fried catfish and this smoky tomato-inflected soup with a surprising kick. Catfish is low in mercury, unlike several types of saltwater fish, and it is high in vitamin D and protein—a three-ounce catfish fillet can provide one-third of your daily protein intake.

- 1 dried guajillo chili
- 1 dried ancho chili
- 4 catfish fillets, cut into 2-inch chunks
- 2 teaspoons sea salt
- 1 teaspoon freshly ground black pepper
- ¼ cup olive oil
- 3 carrots, cut into medium dice
- 3 celery stalks, cut into medium dice
- 1 red onion, diced
- 6 garlic cloves, coarsely chopped
- 6 Roma tomatoes, diced
- 3 red potatoes, halved
- 2 jalapeño peppers, stemmed, seeded, and sliced
- 1 fresh California bay leaf
- 1 teaspoon dried Mexican oregano
- 4 cups fish stock or water
- Small bunch of fresh cilantro, coarsely chopped, for garnish

▶ Steep the guajillo and ancho chilies in 1 cup boiling water for 10 minutes. Transfer the chilies and water to a food processor and pulse until smooth.

▶ Season all sides of the catfish with the salt and pepper.

▶ Heat the oil in a large stockpot over medium heat. Add the carrots, celery, and onions and sauté for 3 to 4 minutes, until they begin to soften. Add the garlic and sauté for 1 minute more to allow the garlic to bloom.

▶ Stir in the chili sauce from the food processor, the tomatoes, potatoes, jalapeños, bay leaf, oregano, and fish stock. Bring the stew to a boil, then add the catfish. Reduce the heat to low and simmer for 20 minutes, or until the catfish is cooked through.

▶ Serve steaming bowls of this stew with a garnish of fresh cilantro and a slab of Roasted Squash Blossom Cornbread (page 119).

▶ Store any leftover stew in an airtight container in the refrigerator for up to 3 days.

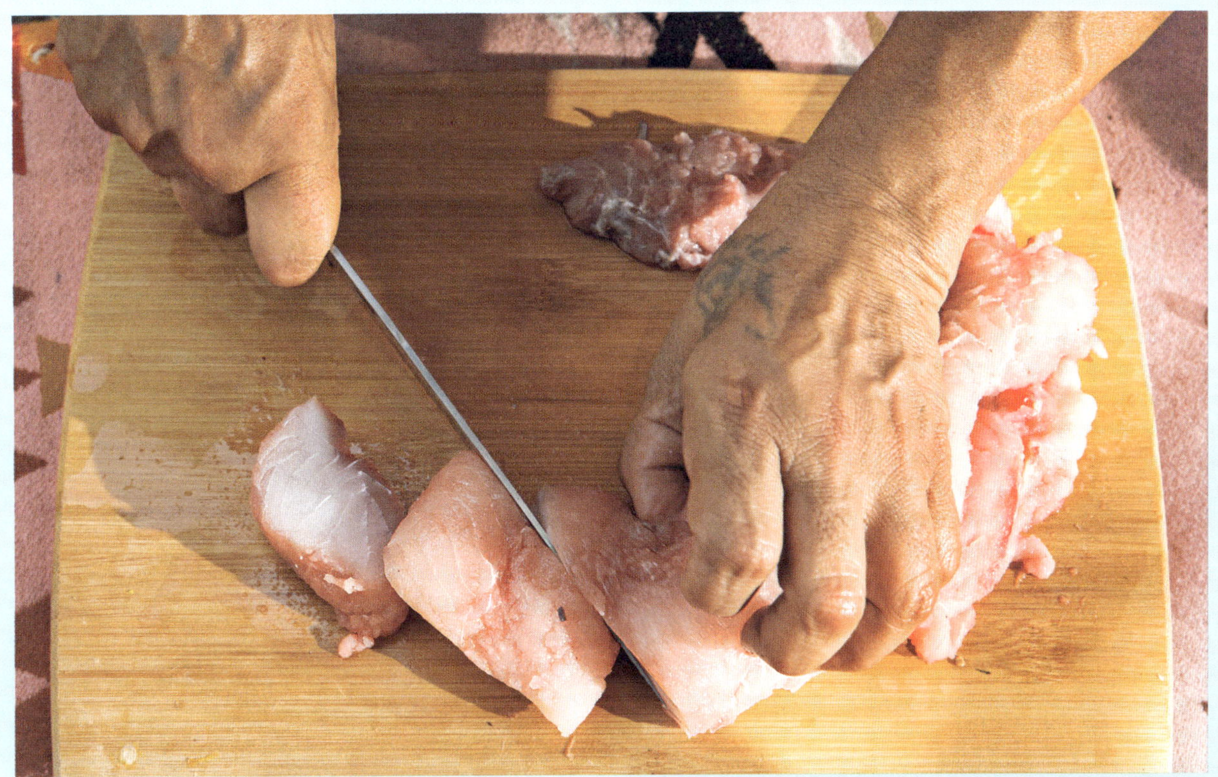

TROUT WITH BERRY COMPOTE

Chaakisii Memeethaki Miinaki

SERVES 4 This recipe can be made with either trout or salmon (see the variation, page 236). Trout is both a fresh- and saltwater fish, depending on the species. It is generally a mild white fish that can be a gateway for someone leery of seafood, while salmon is strong both in color and flavor. Both fish stand up well to the sweet berries—ideal for summer. The creamy-crisp Wild Rice Cakes (page 256), with their bit of earthiness, offer a nice complement, especially when brightened by a side of roasted sweet peppers.

FOR THE BERRY COMPOTE

¼ cup fresh blueberries, plus more for serving

¼ cup fresh blackberries, plus more for serving

¼ cup fresh raspberries, plus more for serving

1 tablespoon pure maple syrup

1 teaspoon blue cornmeal

FOR THE TROUT

3 tablespoons sunflower oil

1 (1-pound trout fillet), cut into 4 (4-ounce) fillets

1 teaspoon sea salt

½ teaspoon freshly ground black pepper

To make the berry compote

- Bring the blueberries, blackberries, raspberries, maple syrup, and ¼ cup water to a simmer in a large saucepan over medium-low heat, stirring occasionally. Reduce the heat to low and continue to simmer for 7 to 10 minutes, stirring occasionally, until the berries have softened and begun to break apart.
- Stir the cornmeal into the berries and cook for another 5 minutes, or until the sauce slightly thickens. Cover to keep warm.

To make the trout

- Heat the oil in a large skillet over medium heat.
- Season the trout fillets with the salt and pepper. Place the fillets, skin-side down, in the hot oil. Cook the trout for 2 to 3 minutes, until the skin is crisp and golden and the flesh flakes. Flip the fillets and cook for 3 minutes more.
- Serve the fillets with a bright, glossy dollop of berry compote, with fresh berries on top.

Notes

Instead of serving the trout in fillet form, present as a whole fish for dramatic effect.

Preheat the oven to 400° F. Coat a shallow baking dish with 1 tablespoon of sunflower oil and brush the fish with the remaining oil.

Season the inside and outside of the fish with the salt and pepper. Lay the fish inside the dish and pour in a couple tablespoons of warm water.

Bake the fish in the preheated oven for 20 minutes, until the fish flakes easily with a fork and the skin is crisp.

VARIATION

SALMON

3 tablespoons olive oil

4 (6-ounce) salmon fillets

Sea salt and freshly ground black pepper

Berry Compote (page 235)

▸ Heat the olive oil in a 12-inch skillet over medium-high heat.

▸ Season fillets all over with salt and pepper. Lay the fillets, flesh-side down, in the skillet and cook for 8 minutes. Flip the fillets and cook for another 5 to 8 minutes, until the skin is crispy and the salmon is cooked almost through.

▸ Transfer the fillets to individual plates and let them rest for 5 minutes.

▸ When ready to serve, spoon the berry compote over the fillets and sprinkle with the reserved berries.

GOOD MEDICINE

More and more, medical researchers are studying food for its preventive benefits. They have learned in recent years just how important eating fish—especially oily fish high in omega-3 fatty acids, such as salmon, halibut, and trout—is to brain function, especially to the part of the brain responsible for memory in older adults.

WHITE FISH TOSTADAS

Chaakisii Memeethaki Methiikwaki

SERVES 4 These tostadas are a study in contrasts. The colors catch your attention immediately—the tone-on-tone halibut and tepary beans against the neutral shade of the tostadas with flashes of green and purple. The textures and flavors reflect the interplay—the crunch of the shell against the creaminess of the fish and beans; the sparkling salsa and sharp onion tempered by the mildly salty flesh. Just a few clean and simple ingredients offer a sensual experience.

- 1 (8-ounce) halibut or other white fish fillet
- 1 teaspoon sea salt
- ½ cup cooked white tepary beans (see page 43)
- 1 tablespoon olive oil
- 4 homemade tostadas (see page 88)
- ¼ cup Green Chili Salsa (page 121)
- ½ small red onion, thinly sliced, for garnish
- ¼ cup chopped fresh cilantro, for garnish

▸ Preheat the oven to 400°F.

▸ Rinse and pat dry the fillet and sprinkle it with the salt. Place the fillet in an ovenproof baking pan. Bake the fillet for 10 to 12 minutes, until cooked through and flaky.

▸ While the fish cooks, pulse the tepary beans and oil in a food processor until the beans are smooth, with the consistency of hummus. Spread about 2 tablespoons of the beans on each of the 4 tostadas.

▸ When the fish is done, flake it into bite-size chunks and pile 2 ounces on each tostada. Top with about 1 tablespoon of green chili salsa and garnish with the onion and cilantro.

GOOD MEDICINE

Halibut is a firm-fleshed, cold-water fish indigenous to northern Pacific waters around Alaska. Like salmon, it is chock-full of omega-3 fatty acids, but halibut also offers high levels of the antioxidant selenium, which is especially important for thyroid health and metabolism.

SALMON AND WATERCRESS CORNBREAD SANDWICH

Chaakisii Memeethaki Otaatopakooni Piipihskiihi

SERVES 4 If I were to tell my story in the form of a sandwich, this one right here would capture the high points. Cornbread, the foundation, the cornerstone of my Native American heritage; salmon, for my home in Northern California and the sacred waters that carry me back to the sea; berry compote, as gratitude to my beloved first friends in the fields; and the rest, for the bitter and sweet that give life and all its highs and lows robust and wild flavor. Together, these ingredients sing in harmony, and I savor every note.

FOR THE CORNBREAD

1 cup gluten-free all-purpose flour

1 cup yellow cornmeal

¼ cup pure maple sugar (see Resources, page 291)

1 tablespoon baking powder

1 teaspoon sea salt

1 cup oat or pecan milk

½ cup (1 stick) unsalted butter, melted and cooled

1 large duck egg

FOR THE SALMON

1 tablespoon pure maple syrup

2 teaspoons sea salt

4 (4-ounce) salmon fillets

FOR THE SANDWICHES

1 recipe Berry Compote (page 235)

Small bunch of watercress

1 Cherokee Purple tomato, sliced

1 small red onion, sliced

To make the cornbread

- Preheat the oven to 350°F. Butter or oil a 9-inch square baking pan.
- Stir together the flour, cornmeal, maple sugar, baking powder, and salt in a large mixing bowl. Make a well in the center.
- Add the oat milk, butter, and egg to the well, then stir the batter together until all the ingredients are combined.
- Pour the batter into the prepared baking pan. Bake the cornbread for 30 to 35 minutes, until the top is golden brown and the edges have pulled away from the pan.
- Allow the cornbread to cool in the pan on a wire rack for about 20 minutes.

To make the salmon

- After the cornbread comes out of the oven, keep the oven temperature at 350°F. Line a baking sheet with parchment paper.
- Mix the maple syrup and salt together in a bowl. Slather the mixture all over the salmon fillets and lay them on the prepared baking sheet. Bake the salmon for 10 to 15 minutes, until it is opaque and easily flakes.

To assemble the sandwiches

- Cut the cornbread into 4 squares, then cut the squares in half for 4 sandwiches.
- For each sandwich, spread the berry compote on the bottom half, then top with a salmon fillet, sprigs of watercress, a tomato slice, and a red onion slice. Crown with the remaining cornbread half and take a bite!

GOOD MEDICINE

Watercress (*Nasturtium officinale*) features high levels of magnesium and calcium, which are essential minerals for preventing osteoporosis. In addition to eating the spicy watercress leaves, brewing them into a tea to drink will help with liver and kidney issues as well as colds and sinus infections.

SMOKED SALMON DIP WITH RED CHILIES AND CHIPS

Pahteewi Chaakisii Memeethaki Chipitiini

SERVES 4 Break the tired salsa routine with this warm dip that has a smoky backbeat. The chilies and salmon bring the toasty notes. Next time you have friends over for a casual night, surprise them with this departure from the norm.

- 10 dried ancho chilies
- 3 dried New Mexico chilies
- 3 Roma tomatoes, halved
- 1 large white onion, quartered
- 1 jalapeño pepper
- 3 garlic cloves
- 1 tablespoon sea salt
- 1 tablespoon olive oil
- ½ cup agave syrup
- 1 (6-ounce) hot-smoked salmon fillet (see Note, page 146), flaked into bite-size pieces
- 1 recipe homemade tortilla chips (see page 88)

▶ Preheat the oven to 425°F. Line a baking sheet with aluminum foil.

▶ Arrange the ancho chilies, New Mexico chilies, tomatoes, onions, jalapeño, and garlic on the prepared baking sheet. Sprinkle with the salt, drizzle with the oil, and toss to coat. Roast for 20 to 25 minutes, until the tomatoes soften and release their juices.

▶ Let the roasted tomatoes and aromatics rest for 5 minutes, then remove the stems and seeds from the ancho and New Mexico chilies and the jalapeño. (Make sure you wear gloves and do not touch your face.)

▶ Transfer all the roasted goodies to a food processor or blender and add the agave syrup. Purée the ingredients until smooth.

▶ Pour the salsa into a bowl and fold in the flaked salmon. Serve slightly warm with warm homemade tortilla chips.

HOW TO CREATE AN INDIGENOUS FOOD BOARD

My aunt Teresa Ballenger was the ultimate hostess. No glass was ever empty, and there was so much food, everyone went home full and with a plate—or two—of leftovers. Her hospitality and generosity of spirit made such an impression on me that I carry her with me into the restaurant every day and into every event we cater.

I want guests to feel that abundance at a cellular level and to focus not on the history of displacement but on the triumph of resilience—not just in my people but with the longevity and vitality of native ingredients. So, I ask myself, "What would Aunt Teresa do?"

Every dish we serve is a gift from Mother Earth, and she takes joy in our vitality. When I arrange an indigenous food board for galas and parties, I envision myself as Mother Earth showcasing those gifts with hot-smoked salmon (see Note, page 146) and eel, venison sausage, Deer Sticks (page 221), wild rice amaranth maple bars, Gooseberry Jam (page 156), and Seaweed Cakes (page 245) nestled amid fresh seasonal fruits and berries, nuts, and seeds.

SEAWEED CAKES

MAKES 12 My daughters are enrolled members of the Big Valley band of Pomo Indians, a Native American community that has lived in the area around Clear Lake, California, for nearly twelve thousand years. The Pomo and other tribes enjoyed unfettered availability of abalone, clams, oysters, and seaweed—or "tono"—all that time until the 1900s, when much of the land and the Pacific coastline were placed under federal restrictions through government ownership of Fort Bragg and the Point Reyes National Seashore. Protecting these vulnerable areas is important, but access to the shore for Native Americans is not only about seeking sustenance but also performing sacred ceremony. So, when seaweed is gifted to me by the Pomo, I try to honor it by how I cook and serve it. This recipe is for my girls.

- 1 cup yellow cornmeal
- ¼ teaspoon baking powder
- Pinch of sea salt
- 1 teaspoon honey
- ¼ cup finely chopped sustainably harvested and dried seaweed such as nori
- 2 tablespoons sunflower oil

▸ Mix the cornmeal, baking powder, salt, and honey by hand in a large bowl. Gently fold in the dried seaweed. Let the mixture rest for 5 minutes.

▸ Shape the mixture into mini pancakes about 3 inches in diameter. Set them aside on parchment paper or paper towels.

▸ Heat about 1 tablespoon of the oil in a large skillet over medium-high heat. Place three to five seaweed cakes in the skillet about 1 inch apart. You will have to work in batches. Cook the cakes for 3 to 4 minutes on each side, until golden brown and cooked through.

▸ Serve two to three cakes per serving. These are delicious with a generous dollop of Gooseberry Jam (page 156) on top.

A Word About Seaweed

Although I have access to the seaweed gathered from my daughters' tribe that is harvested from the ocean and dried, there are other types of seaweed that will work in this recipe. Nori can be purchased in sheets, strips, flakes, or granules. My recommendation is to get them in sheets or strips and break them apart to your liking, or as flakes. Do not rehydrate before folding into the cake mixture.

4

WILD RICE AND ANCIENT GRAINS

Manoomini Miikieni Okweeminaki

Native American tribes that settled along rivers, lakes, and marshlands harvested the tall grasses that produced wild rice for thousands of years because the rice was nutrient-dense and sustained people during lean winter months when other foods were scarce. Quinoa, spelt, amaranth, sorghum, barley, and other ancient grains grew in abundance throughout North and South America until the nineteenth and twentieth centuries, when European wheat became the dominant cultivated crop of the colonialists and was prioritized by government funding and agricultural policies. To this day, hard red winter and hard red spring wheats account for more than 60 percent of all wheat production in the United States.

I am always aware that I walk on stolen land and that where I live, the Ohlone once lived freely for ten thousand years until the eighteenth century. The Ohlone hunted and gathered within the Bay Area's Valley of the Oaks. A staple of their diet was the acorn from the coast live oak, and they developed a process for leaching the tannic acids from the nuts to make them edible. They most often ground the acorns into a mash or into flour for a chewy bread. A man from the Fresno Mono Nation mills small-batch acorn flour for the restaurant and members of his community. It is an honor for me to bake with something made with his hands.

Flours derived from rice, quinoa, amaranth, and acorn are gluten-free and hold important vitamins and other nutrients that combat inflammation, the cause of so many health problems. By returning to the ancient grains in the indigenous diet, we can address digestive issues, autoimmune disorders, and protect against diabetes and other metabolic disorders that are very harmful to our health. At the same time, we can begin the effort to restore our soils.

WILD RICE AND ANCIENT GRAINS

Manoomini Miikieni Okweeminaki

AMARANTH SALAD

Miikieni Okweeminaki Otaatopakooni

SERVES 4 TO 6 This simple, crisp salad has few ingredients but is bursting with flavor from the trio of tomatoes, onion, and cranberries, which balances acid with sugar naturally. The popped amaranth gives it heft and crunch, and the olive oil and agave impart a fruity quality with a light touch. This salad is the ideal side to a bowl of Roasted Acorn Squash Soup (page 117).

6 cups mixed lettuces and greens, such as butterhead, little gem, arugula, dandelion, spring mix, and watercress

2 cups fresh raspberries

½ cup squash blossoms

½ cup dried cranberries

¼ cup olive oil

¼ cup agave syrup

1 cup popped amaranth, for sprinkling

▸ Toss together the lettuce, raspberries, squash blossoms, cranberries, oil, and agave syrup in a large bowl. Sprinkle the popped amaranth on top. Serve the salad with a hearty soup and cornbread.

Note

To give the salad an even brighter flavor and crunchier texture, add 2 cups Cherokee Yellow tomatoes and 1 small sliced red onion when they are in season.

BERRY, BEET, AND QUINOA SALAD

Miinaki Miinekaanani Otaatopakooni

SERVES 4 This salad is so full of color and texture from the beets and the berries that it is like a work of art. The flavors come in waves: earthy, nutty, fruity, sweet, salty, sour, all without competing. The quinoa, a seed that originated with the Incas in Peru, adds another layer of texture, which is pleasing to the palate, plus protein without fat and a heaping dose of magnesium to help regulate blood sugar. The lime gives a hit of acid without overpowering.

- 1 large red beet, roasted and diced
- 1 large yellow beet, roasted and diced
- 1 small red onion, diced
- 2 cups cooked quinoa (see page 43)
- ½ cup fresh blueberries
- ½ cup fresh blackberries
- ½ cup sliced fresh strawberries
- Juice of 1 lime
- ¼ cup pure maple syrup
- 1 teaspoon sea salt

▸ Toss together the red beets, yellow beets, onions, quinoa, blueberries, blackberries, and strawberries in a large bowl. Add the lime juice, maple syrup, and salt and toss again, making sure the lime, maple syrup, and salt are evenly distributed. Cover and set the bowl in the refrigerator for 2 hours to let the flavors mingle and coalesce.

▸ Serve as a side to the Bison Roast with Chokecherry Rub (page 209), Deer Sticks (page 221), or salmon fillets (see page 236).

Note

If beets are not in season or readily available, this salad still dazzles with color and flavor. Add extra crunch and depth with toasted pecans.

AMARANTH MUSH WITH MAPLE

Miikieni Okweeminaki Thiithapaakwamisi

SERVES 4 The Aztecs began cultivating amaranth around eight thousand years ago. It is a striking plant, about six feet tall with a dramatic ponytail fringe of deep red or flaxen flowers and buds that produce tiny, golden bead-like seeds. These seeds are packaged and sold as whole-grain amaranth, but technically they are not a grain, even though you cook and eat them as if they were. Case in point, this warm, comforting cereal, which will remind you of Cream of Wheat in consistency and taste, although amaranth mush has a nuttier flavor.

- 1 cup whole-grain amaranth
- ½ teaspoon sea salt
- ¼ cup pure maple syrup
- Pumpkin Seed Mix (page 154) and raspberries, for garnish (optional)

▸ Bring the amaranth, salt, and 1 cup water to a boil in a medium saucepan over medium heat. Reduce the heat to low and simmer for 2 to 4 minutes, until the water has been absorbed and the consistency is creamy.

▸ Spoon the mush into 4 bowls and drizzle the maple syrup over the mush. For added texture, sprinkle with the pumpkin seed mix and raspberries (if using).

GOOD MEDICINE

There are about seventy species of amaranth (*Amaranthus*), which is an annual plant. For ancient Indigenous peoples, the plant and its seeds possessed spiritual and ceremonial attributes. Because it is drought-resistant, its cultivation offers opportunities as the climate changes. More important, however, is what amaranth offers the body: high levels of protein and complex carbohydrates that produce energy for muscle development, bone formation, and heart health. One cup of cooked amaranth provides more than 90 percent of the daily recommendation for manganese, a trace element that helps manage blood sugar and metabolism.

WILD RICE CAKES

Manoomini Chaakisii Pahkwesikani

MAKES 8 These wild rice cakes are one of the most popular dishes at the restaurant and one of the most requested by catering clients. They are crisp on the outside, creamy in the middle, and filled with the flavors of autumn. The apple, punctuated with sweet cranberries, provides a little tartness that brightens the zucchini's timidness among the bold flavors. The nuttiness of the pumpkin seed cream only deepens that of the rice.

2 small zucchini, grated and drained

1 Granny Smith apple, grated (see Tip)

1 cup wild rice, cooked according to package instructions

1 cup wild rice flour (see Resources, page 293) or gluten-free all-purpose flour

¼ cup olive oil

¼ cup dried cranberries

¼ cup chopped scallions, white and green parts

1 teaspoon sea salt

½ cup Pumpkin Seed Cream (page 184), for drizzling

▸ Preheat the oven to 350°F. Line a baking sheet with parchment paper or spray with nonstick cooking spray.

▸ Combine the zucchini, apple, wild rice, wild rice flour, oil, cranberries, scallions, and salt in a large bowl. I usually mix by hand so that I can get a feel for the texture and how well the ingredients will hold together. That way I can adjust, such as by adding a little more rice or flour. Let the mixture rest and the flavors meld for 10 minutes.

▸ Use a medium (2 tablespoons) ice-cream scoop to form the cakes. Place them about 1 inch apart on the prepared baking sheet. Bake the cakes for 12 to 15 minutes, until golden brown and lightly crisp on the outside.

▸ Serve warm with a drizzle of pumpkin seed cream.

TIP

Substitute chunky applesauce for the grated apple if you desire a cake with a finer texture.

HAND-HARVESTED WILD RICE PILAF

Manoomini

SERVES 4 TO 6 To get the wild rice I need for the restaurant, I have to place my order at least a year in advance, because wild rice is hand-harvested with a priority for community first and sustainability second to ensure that we do not deplete the source. Wild rice has a much different mouthfeel from typical white or brown rice. The grain is longer, the texture chewier, and the taste is slightly grassy with just a hint of smoke. I like to double down on the rice's earthiness with the addition of mushrooms, then send it soaring with the aromatics. The cranberries punctuate it with short bursts of sweetness.

- 2 cups wild rice
- ½ cup butternut or acorn squash, small diced
- ½ cup dried cranberries
- ¼ cup sliced cremini mushrooms
- ¼ cup sliced scallions, white and green parts
- ¼ cup olive oil
- 1 garlic clove, coarsely chopped
- 1 teaspoon sea salt

▸ Preheat the oven to 350°F.

▸ Place the wild rice in a layer on the bottom of a 9 x 13-inch baking pan. Cover the rice with 2 cups cold water, then sprinkle with the squash, cranberries, mushrooms, scallions, oil, garlic, and salt. Stir to combine.

▸ Cover the baking pan with aluminum foil. Bake the rice mixture for 30 minutes, or until all the water is absorbed and the rice is fluffy. Stir with a fork and serve with the Venison or Turkey Meatballs (page 228).

TIP

When squash are in season, add a cup of cubed, uncooked butternut or acorn squash with the cranberries and mushrooms for added color, texture, and flavor.

GOOD MEDICINE

Wild rice is considered by nutritionists as a whole grain, which means it comes with that valuable dietary fiber that supports weight management and helps control blood sugar without the spike-crash cycle. The protein levels provide fuel, and other micronutrients help reduce triglycerides and cholesterol. So, wild rice is worth its longer cook time.

WILD RICE SALAD

Manoomini Otaatopakooni

SERVES 4 TO 6 For a healthy, easy, quick, and filling lunch or a side to the Sweet Potato Tostadas with Chili Oil and Pumpkin Seed Cream (page 184), you cannot go wrong with this salad. It lends itself to improvisation by adding cooked squash, flaked hot-smoked salmon, turkey meatballs, or fresh seasonal fruits. Have fun and be creative.

- 6 cups spring mix lettuce
- 1 cup cooked wild rice, cooled
- ½ cup dried cranberries
- ¼ cup olive oil
- ¼ cup agave syrup
- 1 teaspoon salt
- ¼ cup chopped scallions, white and green parts, for sprinkling
- ¼ cup popped amaranth, for sprinkling

▶ Toss the lettuce, wild rice, cranberries, oil, agave syrup, and salt in a large bowl. Sprinkle the top with the scallions and amaranth to serve.

ACORN CREPES

Mehtekomini

MAKES 12 While still delicate, acorn crepes offer a little more heft and depth of flavor than those made with all-purpose or pastry flours. These folded pockets of goodness make a lovely breakfast, brunch, or dessert. Here, I serve them with the Berry Compote, but they would be just as tasty with Gooseberry Jam (page 156) and a sprinkling of Pumpkin Seed Mix (page 154) or a drizzle of Maple Cream (page 58). Or, go savory with mashed sweet potatoes and a swath of Pumpkin Seed Cream (page 184). As most people do not own or have access to a crepe maker, these can be made in an 8-inch skillet.

- 2 cups almond or oat milk
- 2 large duck eggs
- 1 cup acorn flour
- 1 cup gluten-free all-purpose flour
- 3 tablespoons unsalted butter, melted and cooled
- 1 tablespoon pure maple sugar (see Resources, page 291)
- ⅛ teaspoon sea salt
- 1 recipe Berry Compote (page 235), for serving

▸ Combine the almond milk, eggs, acorn flour, all-purpose flour, butter, maple sugar, and salt in a food processor and blend until smooth.

▸ Heat an 8-inch skillet over medium heat. Add some butter and let it melt to coat the bottom of the skillet.

▸ Once the butter is melted, pour ¼ cup of the crepe batter into the dead center of the skillet and twirl the skillet until the batter makes a thin circle. Cook for 1 to 2 minutes to set the crepe, then use a heatproof rubber spatula to help flip the crepe. Cook for 30 seconds, or until the crepe is light brown.

▸ Transfer the crepe to a large platter and fold it in half, then in half again, to make a triangle. Repeat the crepe-making process until you have used up the batter and all the crepes have been made. Stack on the platter separated by parchment paper or wax paper.

▸ Place one or two crepes per person on plates with a tablespoon or more of the berry compote. Serve immediately.

Note

While there are Japanese acorn flours available at some specialized markets and online, to find California-milled acorn flour from the Sierra Nevada region, go to the all-female owned Quercus Collective, quercuscollective.com. And soon in Mendocino, California, the Manzanita Cooperative will bring acorn flour and other acorn-based products to the marketplace. Learn more at manzanitacooperative.com.

MAYAN CHOCOLATE AMARANTH CAKE

Mayan Chaakaneti Miikieni Okweeminaki Chaakisii Pahkwesikani

SERVES 6 TO 8 There is a reason the Mayans referred to cacao as the food of the gods as early as 1500 BCE. In its purest form, the spicy drink they made from cacao beans and chilies sealed marriages, was used for offerings, and gave the Mayans energy. These little cakes pack that intense chocolate flavor without the inherent bitterness and without being overly sweet. The cinnamon and vanilla are a nod to chocolate's Mexican and Central American origins.

2 cups Mayan cocoa powder (see Note)

1 cup amaranth flour (see page 81)

1 cup pure maple sugar (see Resources, page 291)

1 teaspoon baking powder

1 teaspoon ground cinnamon

1 teaspoon sea salt

6 large duck eggs, lightly beaten

1 cup sunflower oil

1 teaspoon pure vanilla extract

4 fresh strawberries, sliced, for serving

Edible flowers, for serving

Puffed amaranth, for garnish

▸ Preheat the oven to 350°F. Spray six to eight 1-cup ramekins with nonstick cooking spray. Set the ramekins on a baking sheet.

▸ Mix together the cocoa powder, amaranth flour, maple sugar, baking powder, cinnamon, and salt in a large bowl. Stir in the eggs, oil, and vanilla with a wooden spoon and mix for 2 minutes, or until all the ingredients are incorporated.

▸ Spoon the cake batter into the 4 prepared ramekins. Bake the cakes for 12 to 15 minutes, until set. Cool the cakes on a wire rack for 15 to 20 minutes before serving.

▸ Serve with the strawberries, flowers, and/or a sprinkle of puffed amaranth.

Note

There are multiple online sources for Mayan cocoa powder, but I source for home and restaurant from Che'il Mayan Chocolate in Stann Creek, Belize, where Julio Saqui runs the factory and offers tours. To find out more about Che'il's products and to order, call 501-637-6521. Also, check out their Facebook and Instagram profiles.

CHOCOLATE ACORN COOKIES

Chaakaneti Mehtekomini Kohkisaani

MAKES 24 These cookies are my interpretation of a classic chocolate chip, but with a richer, nuttier flavor courtesy of the acorn flour, which gives the cookies a little nutritional boost of vitamins A and C as well. The combined maple and brown sugars impart caramel notes. Feel free to substitute a gluten-free all-purpose flour alternative to ensure these cookies can be enjoyed by friends with sensitivities.

- 2 cups acorn flour (see Resources, page 291)
- 1 cup all-purpose flour
- 1 teaspoon baking soda
- ½ teaspoon baking powder
- 1 teaspoon sea salt
- 1 cup (2 sticks) unsalted butter
- 1 cup pure maple sugar (see Resources, page 291)
- 1 cup (packed) brown sugar
- 2 teaspoons pure vanilla extract
- 2 large duck eggs, lightly beaten
- 2 cups semisweet chocolate chips

▸ Preheat the oven to 350°F. Line a baking sheet with parchment paper.

▸ Whisk together the acorn flour, all-purpose flour, baking soda, baking powder, and salt in a large bowl.

▸ Beat the butter, maple sugar, and brown sugar in the bowl of a stand mixer fitted with the paddle attachment on medium-high speed until the butter is light and airy. Beat in the vanilla, then add the eggs and beat until thoroughly combined. Scrape down the sides of the bowl periodically to ensure all the ingredients are mixed well.

▸ Reduce the mixer speed to low, add the flour mixture, and mix until the dough holds together. Stir in the chocolate chips.

▸ Use a medium (2 tablespoons) ice-cream scoop to place balls of dough 2 inches apart on the prepared baking sheet. Bake the cookies for 8 to 10 minutes, until the edges look dry and crisp and you can just smell the chocolate. Let the cookies cool on the baking sheet for 2 minutes before transferring them to a wire rack to cool completely.

ACORN MUFFINS

Mehtekomini Chaakisii Pahkwesikani

MAKES 12 For breakfasts or snacks, these dense, lightly sweet muffins keep you full and energized. Paired with Blue Corn Mush with Mixed Berries (page 72), you will be able to take on anything life throws at you.

- 1 cup acorn flour (see Resources, page 291)
- 1 cup all-purpose flour
- 1 large duck egg
- ¼ cup pecan or oat milk
- ¼ cup honey
- ¼ teaspoon baking powder
- 1 teaspoon sea salt
- 1 recipe Maple Cream (page 58), for serving

▸ Preheat the oven to 350°F. Line a 12-cup muffin tin with parchment liners or spray with nonstick cooking spray.

▸ Combine the acorn flour, all-purpose flour, egg, pecan milk, honey, baking powder, and salt in the bowl of a stand mixer fitted with the paddle attachment on medium speed for about 3 minutes. The batter should be thick and smooth.

▸ Fill the prepared muffin cups about three-quarters full with the batter. Bake the muffins for 12 minutes, or until golden brown. Let the muffins cool for 10 minutes before removing them from the tin and setting them on a wire rack to cool completely.

▸ Serve with a drizzle of maple cream over the tops.

5

BEVERAGES AND TEAS

Ochiikaapowi

Because I am committed to creating a place of health and healing at Wahpepah's Kitchen and because so many people within my family endured alcoholism and substance abuse, I do not serve alcohol at my restaurant. But by no means am I opposed to sparkling, effervescent waters and fun combinations of ingredients to create tasty beverages that lift the spirits. And you will be surprised how vinegar can be transformed into a drink that quenches your thirst and tantalizes your taste buds while also doing your body good.

Throughout the book under the headings of Good Medicine, I have shared how different plants, herbs, fruits, and vegetables can also be enjoyed as teas. Teas and tinctures have been brewed by people across time and place to instill good health, good mood, and, in many cases, good conversation. My favorites, of course, include blackberries.

BEVERAGES AND TEAS

Ochiikaapowi

PRICKLY PEAR SPARKLER

Mehskopwaakaa

SERVES 4 I make batch after batch of this mocktail during that brief window of three to four weeks in August and September when prickly pear fruits are available. The fruit can be enjoyed fresh or boiled into jams and jellies or mashed. It is stunning with its vibrant magenta color, yet it is subtle in flavor, more like an early-season watermelon or honeydew melon than a pear.

4 small prickly pear fruits, peeled

3 cups lemon-lime soda

▸ Bring the prickly pears and about 1 cup water (enough to just cover the fruit) to a boil in a medium saucepan over medium-high heat. Remove from the heat and let the mixture steep for 30 minutes.

▸ Mash the pear mixture with the back of a wooden spoon or with a potato masher, then strain the mash through a fine-mesh sieve into a bowl, more than once if necessary, until you have a clear magenta-colored syrup.

▸ Divide the syrup among four 12-ounce tumblers. Fill the tumblers with ice and top them off with the lemon-lime soda. Stir and enjoy this late-summer delight.

GOOD MEDICINE

Like all true cacti, the prickly pear (*Opuntia humifusa*) is indigenous to the Americas, growing abundantly in dry desert climates such as in Mexico, the southwestern United States, and portions of the Caribbean. The entire plant is edible once you remove the spines. Native Americans performed this task by rubbing the plant's fleshy pads, or nopales, and fruit in sand. According to the American Indian Health and Diet Project, Native Americans heated the nopales and used them as compresses on swollen joints and injuries. They cut them open and rubbed the pads on wounds, and they made candy and an early, early version of chewing gum. Because of the fruit's high fiber and antioxidant compounds, consuming prickly pear can help lower blood pressure.

PINEAPPLE ELDERBERRY TEA

Miinaki Ochiikaapowi

SERVES 4 This tea benefits from the gifts of red and blue elderberries, bushes with flowers that bloom into small but mighty immune boosters that grow along the California coast. The blue elderberries offer high antiviral compounds that help minimize the impacts of colds. I especially turn to elderberry tea during flu season. The bromelain in pineapple protects against internal inflammation that leads to heart disease and osteoarthritis. Together, the pineapple and elderberry make a sassy combination.

2 cups fresh pineapple juice

1 cup fresh or frozen elderberries

¼ cup pure maple syrup

3 tablespoons dried hibiscus flowers

▸ Bring the pineapple juice, elderberries, maple syrup, hibiscus flowers, and 2 cups water to a boil in a medium saucepan over medium heat, stirring occasionally. Remove from the heat and let the ingredients steep for 15 minutes.

▸ Strain the pineapple elderberry tea through a fine-mesh sieve into a teapot or pitcher. Serve hot or cold.

SÉKA HILLS POMEGRANATE SPARKLER

Meskwaaki Eteeteeki

SERVES 1 In the rural Capay Valley of Northern California, the Native-owned farm Séka Hills produces the lush olive oils I use for cooking and salad dressings, and the thick, rich syrups derived from pressing fruits and allowing them to age into piquant balsamic vinegars as well. These vinegars make tangy sparklers similar to kombucha, but they also have surprising benefits from their high acetic acid content, which acts as an antimicrobial that aids in digestion and blood sugar management.

3 tablespoons pomegranate balsamic vinegar (see Resources, page 291)

2 tablespoons pure maple syrup

1 cup sparkling water

▸ Mix the vinegar and maple syrup in a pint glass. Fill the glass with ice and pour in the sparkling water. Stir and enjoy the healing refreshment.

Notes

Substitute 3 tablespoons elderberry or fig balsamic vinegar for the pomegranate balsamic vinegar.

Substitute 2 tablespoons agave syrup or honey for the maple syrup.

HIBISCUS TEA

Peeskoneiihi Ochiikaapowi

SERVES 4 Hibiscus is not native to the Americas—it originated in the tropical climates of Africa and Asia. It came to this part of the world through the Caribbean during the 1500s and the transatlantic slave trade, when enslaved Africans brought with them seeds and food traditions that changed the landscape of cooking in the Americas forever. Red drinks are culturally significant in the African diaspora, including among Oakland's large population. This drink leans in to that shared indigenous knowledge of drawing from plants their highest and best uses—and this tea is one of them. Hibiscus flowers infuse the water with a deep red pigment and citrusy-floral note that pairs well with the spice of cinnamon and cloves. This drink may be enjoyed hot or iced.

½ cup dried hibiscus flowers
¼ cup pure maple syrup
1 cinnamon stick
1 whole clove

▸ Bring the hibiscus flowers, maple syrup, cinnamon, clove, and 4 cups water to a boil in a medium saucepan over medium heat, stirring occasionally. Remove from the heat and let the ingredients steep for 5 minutes.

▸ Strain the hibiscus tea through a fine-mesh sieve into a teapot or pitcher. Serve hot or cold.

TIP

Punch it up with 3 tablespoons pomegranate balsamic vinegar (see Resources, page 291).

GOOD MEDICINE

Like other brilliantly colored plants, hibiscus overflows with anthocyanins, flavonoids that give cherries, red cabbage, plums, and other red, purple, and blue fruits, vegetables, and plants their hue. Anthocyanins are antimicrobial powerhouses that can strengthen vision, boost brain health to stave off memory loss, and slow cancer cell growth. It makes sense, then, that the first people were naturally attracted to the most colorful plants for foods.

BLACKBERRY SAGE TEA

Meekateethichik Miinaki Otaatopakwi Ochiikaapowi

SERVES 4 We bring huge coolers full of this tea to our catering events, especially the Stanford Powwow every spring. This refreshing tea sells out as folks spend all day outdoors celebrating Native American heritage through dance, drumming, chanting, and ceremonies. Because blackberries have a purple grapelike flavor, this tea tastes almost like a punch, but the sweetness is tempered by the sage, which gives it a pleasant, herbaceous quality.

1 cup fresh blackberries

3 fresh sage leaves

1 tablespoon pure maple syrup

▸ Bring the blackberries, sage leaves, maple syrup, and 4 cups water to a boil in a medium saucepan over medium heat, stirring occasionally. Remove from the heat and let the ingredients steep for 15 minutes.

▸ Strain the blackberry sage tea through a fine-mesh sieve into a teapot or pitcher. Serve hot or cold.

WILD MINT TEA

Ceyaka Ochiikaapowi

SERVES 4 Have you ever been told to suck on a peppermint when you had a tummy ache or felt nauseated? That comes from indigenous knowledge, because Native Americans gathered wild mint from riverbanks and marshes and dried the leaves for a tea to soothe stomach issues. The fragrant menthol compounds and antibacterials are also good for lung health. Beyond these healthy properties, however, "ceyaka," the Lakota word for mint tea, is refreshing either hot or cold.

1 cup dried wild mint

- Bring the wild mint and 4 cups water to a boil in a medium saucepan over medium heat, stirring occasionally. Remove from the heat and let the ingredients steep for 15 minutes.
- Strain the wild mint tea through a fine-mesh sieve into a teapot or pitcher. Serve hot or cold.

AFTERWORD

This book began with a prayer. It ends with an offering.

Throughout most of my life, I have moved between many worlds—the urban indigenous one of Oakland into which I was born and where I have made my home, and the quiet rolling plains of Oklahoma, where most of my family returned to live among the Kickapoo and the Sac and Fox. I am at peace on busy city streets as much as I am in the redwoods along the Pacific shore, the places that are sacred to the Pomo—the tribe of my daughters. This land is sacred to me as well.

I will always be grateful to my uncle Bill for encouraging pride in my Native American heritage. His guidance, his passion, his advocacy—I know his example, and that of my aunties, is the spark that lit my fire for food sovereignty. Still, there always was half of me that felt unknown. Only recently have I learned more about my biological father. There is a deeper story here, about how the blood that courses through my body tells the fraught story of this country, how the food I prepare taps into the reservoir of wisdom that came before colonialism, how my father's food traditions tell the story of what came after, how both are complicated and messy and beautiful and the path toward healing fractured people.

COCONUT CORN CAKE

Methiikwaki Chaakisii Pahkwesikani

SERVES 8 TO 12 This final recipe departs from my no-dairy, no-processed-sugar, precolonial cooking ethos. Instead, it honors a part of me I am now beginning to learn about. It is based on a coconut cake that was awarded as a prize and served as the centerpiece of celebrations in Black traditions. The added texture from the corn in the batter puts a bit of me into the mix. This cake is an offering to the ancestors.

A'ho.

FOR THE CAKE

2 cups cake flour

1 cup white cornmeal

1 tablespoon baking powder

½ teaspoon sea salt

1 cup (2 sticks) unsalted butter, at room temperature

2 cups granulated sugar

1 cup coconut milk

12 large egg whites, beaten to stiff peaks

FOR THE FROSTING

6 ounces cream cheese, at room temperature

1 teaspoon coconut extract

3½ cups confectioners' sugar

2 cups unsweetened shredded coconut

To make the cake

▸ Preheat the oven to 350°F. Butter and flour a 9 x 13-inch baking pan or spray with nonstick cooking spray. Line the bottom of the pan with parchment paper.

▸ Whisk together the cake flour, cornmeal, baking powder, and salt in a large bowl.

▸ Cream the butter in the bowl of a stand mixer fitted with the paddle attachment on medium-high speed for about 3 minutes, until the butter is pale and smooth. Beat the granulated sugar into the butter for about 5 minutes, until thoroughly incorporated and no longer gritty.

▸ Reduce the mixer speed to medium, then alternate adding the flour mixture and the coconut milk until the batter is smooth. Scrape down the sides of the bowl periodically to make sure all the ingredients are incorporated. Gently fold the egg whites into the cake batter until there are no more white streaks.

▸ Spread the batter evenly into the prepared baking pan. Bake the cake for 30 to 40 minutes, until golden brown and the sides of the cake have pulled away from the pan. If the surface of the cake springs back at your touch, it is ready to completely cool on a wire rack.

To make the frosting

▸ Once the cake is cooled, beat the cream cheese and coconut extract in the clean bowl of the stand mixer fitted with the paddle attachment on medium-high speed for about 2 minutes, until smooth. Reduce the speed to low and add the confectioners' sugar, about 1 cup at a

time, making sure the sugar is completely incorporated before adding the next cup.

▸ Frost the cooled cake while it is still in the pan and sprinkle the top generously with the shredded coconut.

▸ Cut the cake into squares and serve with a lovely cup of hot Wild Mint Tea (page 280).

ACKNOWLEDGMENTS

This book exists because of the love of so many people.

I am indebted to the elders and ancestors who gave me life and sustained me. To my mother, Beverly Wahpepah: I literally would not be here without you. To Aunt Teresa Bellanger: Thank you for the lessons in food and hospitality, and how to be a strong woman. To Aunt Carleta: for showing me how to love. Thank you to my grandmother Cecilia Jennings, who gave me the gift of patience. To Grandfather Eugene Makaseah, who showed me the sacredness of the land, teaching me how to grow, forage, and hunt. To my Oklahoma cousins Carol Wahpepah and Leslie Wahpepah Barse, who adopted me after my mother's death and filled in so many parts of my family history. And to Carol's husband, Dan Harris, whose beautiful pottery appears in these pages. To the extended family of cousins: Ruth Ann, Kathy, Nick, Red Sky. To my nephews and niece—Robert Osife, Tara Wallace, Ryan Wallace: I always want the best for you.

To Aunt Carol Wahpepah: You introduced me to art and culture by taking me to museums and performances, and because of you, I see beauty. I also understand commitment to community through your lifelong dedication to the American Indian Child Resource Center and the Intertribal Friendship House. Many thanks to Uncle Richard and Auntie Arvella Movescamp and Auntie Lupe and Uncle David for your unconditional love. To Corrina Gould and Auntie Johnella LaRose: You are fierce in your work to rematriate lands and care for your families. I am grateful to be among the ones you fight for. Your belief in me has given me wings, as has the Native American Health Center—Martin Waukazoo and staff were the first ones to provide support and push me into bigger things.

The Bay Area Native community has always had my back.

As have Harry and Marie Hopper, my daughters' grandparents, who have been there for us in countless ways. My daughters have grown up with me, worked beside me. The success of Wahpepah's Kitchen is as much theirs as mine. They have been integral members of the Wahpepah's Kitchen and catering family—to whom I owe so much gratitude for being ambassadors of the restaurant's mission and indigenous foodways. That gratitude extends to John Lozano.

I am indebted to The Cultural Conservancy and the Native American food producers who grow traditional ingredients and entrust me with their tribal foods. I am equally inspired by the Indigenous chefs who paved the way for me—all the women who cook for their communities—and my fellow food warriors who possess such strong commitments to their communities and food sovereignty: Sean Sherman, Dr. Claudia Serrato, Nephi Craig, Brian Yazzie, Marlene Aguilar, and Karlos Baca.

Many thanks to the creative team who helped bring this book to life. First and foremost, my agent Sally Ekus. We share the same birthday. We will always be connected. My co-writer, Amy Paige Condon, has a special gift for making things come to life. I have no words for you and your support with this book. Editor Dervla Kelly, who understood my vision for this book and led the team at Rodale to make it a reality. Photographer Clay Williams, along with stylists Jillian Knox and Marina Freytes, and photography assistants Shameika and Shantara Ejiasi, I am stunned by the way you captured this spirit of our food. Cosita Photo Studio and Prop House provided the perfect setting for us to work. Many thanks to Robin Meel of the Coast Miwok and Pomo Tribe, who worked with the Pomo Basket Society for the loan of historic native baskets for our photo shoots. Luke, a member of the Cheyenne River Sioux Tribe, and his wife Linda Black Elk provided essential guidance about the medicinal and ceremonial attributes of plants and other ingredients. To my niece, Nani Hopper, thanks for doing double duty as my sous chef during the shoot and holding it down at the restaurant. To Shelly Wahpepah, Paulina Wahpepah, and Mosiah Salazar Bluecloud for keeping the language of the Kickapoo alive.

We are all a community now. We are forever family.

LANDBACK
TOUR 2022
GLEN FALLS, NY
PORTAND, ME
LAKE PLACID, NY
CHARLESTON, WV
HAMPTON, VA
BALTIMORE, MD
RICHMOND, VA
HARTFORD, CT
PROVIDENCE, RI
ERIE, PA
MEADOWLANDS, NJ-NY
LONG ISLAND, NY
EVANSVILLE, IN
CARBONDALE, IL
PEORIA, IL
FORT WAYNE, IN
LEXINGTON, KY
DETROIT, MI
BATTLE CREEK, MI
MILWAUKEE, WI
AMES, IA
MADISON, WI
CEDAR RAPIDS, IA
WICHITA, KS
NORMAN, OK
SHREVEPORT, LA
AUSTIN, TX
SAN ANTONIO, TX
TUCSON, AZ
LOS ANGELES, CA
THE ORIGINAL LANDLORDS

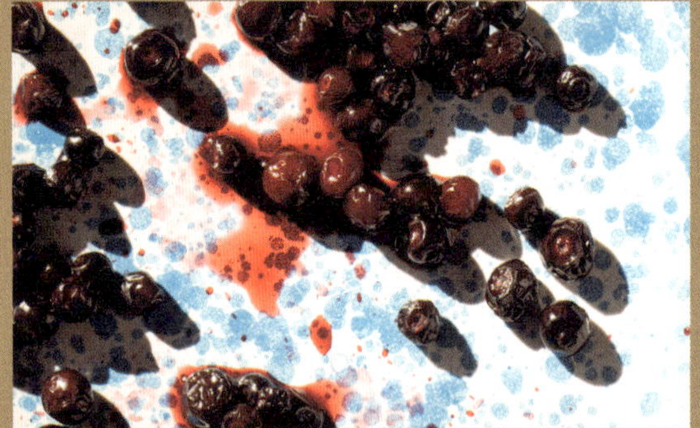

NIKE AIR

RESOURCES

WHERE TO FIND INGREDIENTS BY NATIVE FOOD GROWERS AND PRODUCERS

Food sovereignty involves foraging, growing, and producing whole and healthy indigenous foods using heirloom seeds and with traditional ecological knowledge—the old ways, with the wisdom of the ancestors. It is the way to reclaim our land, our livelihoods, our health, and our identities, while also healing the Earth. We do not assume that one tribe's seeds are our own to take and use as we please; instead, we await the sacred gift, the blessing, and the honor to share our seeds with one another. We pray over them, seeking guidance for how to use them for the greatest good. We take care of our elders and our communities first, and then we share our bounty broadly to help feed and sustain one another.

I and the Native food producers I work with want to make native ingredients the norm rather than the exception. Food is good medicine, and we want to foster strong, mutually beneficial relationships with plants, animals, and the land. Beginning in the 1800s, the U.S. government denied our inherent human right to grow and eat our foods when we were forcibly removed from our lands. Seed by seed, we are reintroducing the corn, squash, beans, rice, and wild greens that have always grown on these lands sustainably so that we will not lose, again, our physical and mental health, our cultures, or ourselves to disease and displacement. By using ingredients grown, harvested, and produced by Indigenous peoples, we—and you—are supporting food sovereignty and Native American economies, and keeping our traditions alive.

Bow & Arrow Brand
Towaoc, Colorado
bowandarrowbrand.com
The Ute Mountain Ute Tribe grow blue, yellow, and white corn on a 7,700-acre sustainable farm, where they also grow alfalfa and raise cattle. The growers harvest, mill, and package the corn right there on the reservation.

Cheyenne River Buffalo Company
Eagle Butte, South Dakota
wsidemeats.com
The Cheyenne River Lakota Sioux revived the nearly extinct buffalo into one of the largest tribally owned and managed herds in the nation. Wahpepah's Kitchen purchases our steaks, roasts, and ground meats from the Cheyenne River tribe.

Dynamite Hill Farms
L'Anse, Michigan
dynamitehillfarms@gmail.com
On thirty acres near Lake Superior, Jerry Jondreau and Katy Bresette have reintroduced regenerative growing and harvesting techniques to bring back Ojibwe traditions and foods. Their maple sugar, maple vinegar, and maple syrup sweeten many of the recipes in this book.

Intertribal Agriculture Council (Indian Ag)
Billings, Montana
indianagfoods.org/directory
American Indian Foods, under the auspices of the Intertribal Agriculture Council, provides a platform for Native American food producers to get their goods and wares out into the world. The products showcased through this program are cultivated on Native American lands and waters, according to the traditions of tribal cultures. This organization provided the path for me to sell and distribute my wild rice amaranth maple bars outside of the restaurant. When I catered the Indian Ag annual conference at the Palms Casino Resort in Las Vegas in 2023, I was introduced to many new Native food producers; the experience expanded what I could serve in my restaurant and who I could support.

North American Traditional Indigenous Food Systems (NATIFS)
Minneapolis, Minnesota
natifs.org
Founded by Sioux chef Sean Sherman, NATIFS is both a commercial kitchen and culinary training hub with the mission to reintegrate native foods into tribal communities throughout North America and serve as an incubator for Native American cookery and innovation. The Indigenous Food Lab (IFL) provides in-person and online classes on how to cook with native ingredients. The IFL market offers grab-and-go and made-to-order meals as well as provides for sale products made by Indigenous peoples throughout the Americas, from wild rice hand-gathered around the Great Lakes to single-source chocolate from Ecuador.

Passamaquoddy Maple and Passamaquoddy Wild Blueberry Co.
Jackson, Maine, and Columbia Falls, Maine
passamaquoddymaple.com and pquoddyberries.com
Members of the Passamaquoddy tribe of Maine have been harvesting maple sap and blueberries for centuries. The tribe makes small-batch syrups as well as sugar and candies. The tiny, nutrient-packed blueberries grow wild on two thousand acres of barrens and are hand-harvested.

Quapaw Cattle Company
Miami, Oklahoma
quapawtribe.com/511/Quapaw-Cattle-Company
In the far northeastern corner of Oklahoma, past the casino and golf course, the Quapaw Nation operates a 5,755-acre ranch with grazing lands for cows and buffalo, and a row crop farm that provides produce for the community, a farmers' market, food hub, and farm store.

Ramona Farms
Sacaton, Arizona
ramonafarms.com
The heritage black, white, brown, and cranberry beans and heirloom corns I use at home, in catering, and at the restaurant come from Ramona Farms, a forty-year-old Akimel O'odham desert farm on the land of the Gila River Indian Community.

Red Lake Nation Inc. Brands
Nawapo online marketplace
Bemidji, Minnesota
nawapo.com
The Red Lake band of the Chippewa remain on the aboriginal lands around the Lower and Upper Red Lake in northern Minnesota near the Canadian border. This land and the more than 280,000 acres of waterways was never ceded in the 1880s and remains held and managed by the tribe. In the fringes along the lakes and rivers, members of the Red Lake band gather wild rice, pick wild berries for jams and jellies, and gather wild and cultivated herbs, grasses, and flowers for herbal teas.They are a source for wild rice flour and chokecherry patties.

Sakari Farms and Botanicals
Bend, Oregon, and Tumalo, Oregon
sakarifarms.com
When I need squash blossoms, herbal teas, and edible flowers, I go to Spring Alaska Schreiner, the Inupiaq owner of Sakari Farms and Botanicals. The farm is also home to the Pacific Northwest Tribal Seed Bank, which forms the basis of research and education and is for tribal members only.

Salmon King Fisheries
Warm Springs, Oregon
salmonkingfisheries.com
In business since 2011, this Native woman–owned business sells fresh, frozen, and smoked sockeye and coho salmon, as well as steelhead, from the Columbia River near Warm Springs, Oregon.

Séka Hills
Brooks, California
sekahills.com
The Yocha Dehe Wintun Nation presses exceptional olive oils, harvests seasonal wildflower honeys, and produces intense fruity vinegars (including a pomegranate balsamic vinegar) in the fertile Capay Valley of Northern California.

Spirit Lake Native Farms
Sawyer, Minnesota
spiritlakenativefarms.com
Not far from Lake Superior, this small, family-run Native-owned farm produces two of my favorite ingredients: hand-harvested wild rice and pure maple syrup. I have to order the amount of wild rice needed for the restaurant at least a year ahead, because the wild rice is hand-harvested from the lakes around the Anishinaabe/Ojibwe lands. The maple syrup is boiled over wood fires, just as the elders and ancestors always did it.

SweetGrass Trading Company
Winnebago, Nebraska
sweetgrasstradingco.com
This purveyor of Native American–produced goods carries smoked salmon, sausages, smoked cedar salts, and other seasonings, teas, coffees, and so many more ingredients to support Indigenous growers and artisans and to create authentically Native American dishes.

Temalpakh Farm
Coachella, California
temalpakhfarm.com
"Temalpakh" means "from the earth," and that is the commitment from this organic-certified farm planted and harvested by the Augustine band of the Cahuilla Indians. The farm boxes of seasonal produce offer nutrition to both community and wholesale buyers. The guided farm tours offer education about the farm's sustainable ecological practices.

Tocabe Indigenous Marketplace
Denver, Colorado
shoptocabe.com
Founded by Ben Jacobs, a member of the Osage Nation, and Matt Chandra, Tocabe is a brick-and-mortar eatery in North Denver, Colorado; sells ready-made meals; and is a purveyor of Native-produced ingredients. Every time someone orders something from the Tocabe Indigenous Marketplace, the company donates ingredients to Native communities across America to help rebuild "the original American food system."

Yakama Nation Farms
Toppenish, Washington
ynfarms.com
The tribal bands of the Yakama have lived in the Columbia River Valley of Washington State for thousands of years. The Yakama Indian Reservation totals more than one million acres in this area and is home to Yakama Nation Farms, which provides fresh, organic produce wholesale to markets and restaurants, and seasonal produce boxes to community members. They are known for their bell and hot peppers, pumpkins, squash, and greens. The farm was founded by the Inaba brothers, Japanese immigrants who moved to the reservation in 1907. After three generations, the Inaba family sold the farm to the Yakama Nation in 2022.

OTHER RESOURCES

American Indian Child Resource Center
aicrc.org

American Indian Film Festival
instagram.com/aifisf

Cultural Conservancy
nativeland.org

Intertribal Friendship House
ifhurbanrez.org

Kickapoo Tribe of Oklahoma
kickapootribeofoklahoma.com

La Cocina (nonprofit)
lacocinasf.org

Native American Food Sovereignty Alliance (NAFSA)
nativefoodalliance.org

Native American Health Center
nativehealth.org

Red Nation International Film Festival (RNIFF)
rednationff.com

Sogorea Te' Land Trust
sogoreate-landtrust.org

Stanford Powwow
stanfordpowwow.com

ESSENTIAL READINGS

Joseph, Leigh. *Held by the Land Deck: 45 Ways to Use Indigenous Plants for Healing & Nourishment.* New York: Wellfleet Press, 2024.

Luger, Chesley, and Thosh Collins. *The Seven Circles: Indigenous Teachings for Living Well.* New York: HarperOne, 2022.

Orange, Tommy. *There There: A Novel.* New York: Alfred A. Knopf, 2018.

———. *Wandering Stars: A Novel.* New York: Alfred A. Knopf, 2024.

Sherman, Sean, with Beth Dooley. *The Sioux Chef's Indigenous Kitchen.* Minneapolis: University of Minnesota Press, 2017.

Shimer, Porter. *Healing Secrets of the Native Americans: Herbs, Remedies, and Practices that Restore the Body, Refresh the Mind, and Rebuild the Spirit.* New York: Black Dog & Leventhal, 2004.

INDEX

NOTE: Page references in *italics* indicate photographs.

C

D

E

F

G

H

I

J

K

L

M

N

O

P

Q

R

T

V

ABOUT THE AUTHOR

Whose land do we walk on?

This question is the first one Chef Crystal Wahpepah asks of any place she cooks. The answer matters because Crystal is a true Indigenous food warrior and the first Native woman to own a restaurant in Northern California. A member of the Kickapoo Nation of Oklahoma, Wahpepah grew up in and around the urban Indigenous communities of Oakland, where her Fruitvale Transit Village restaurant, Wahpepah's Kitchen, reclaims Native foodways and connects guests to the vibrant, nourishing bounty of Native foods and intertribal cultures. By serving Kickapoo Chili, salmon, and Three Sisters Salad among other indigenous dishes, Crystal honors the land and waters and the sustenance they provide while creating community and helping her community heal.

Crystal is an inductee into the Native American Almanac, was a finalist for the James Beard Emerging Chef Award, and has appeared on Food Network's *Chopped* and *Beating Bobby Flay.* She serves as a U.S. State Department culinary ambassador and has catered for the Academy of Motion Picture Arts and Sciences and for the American Indian Film Festival.